Shojo Beat

BABY & Me

Vol. 9

Story & Art by **Marimo Ragawa**

Table of Contents

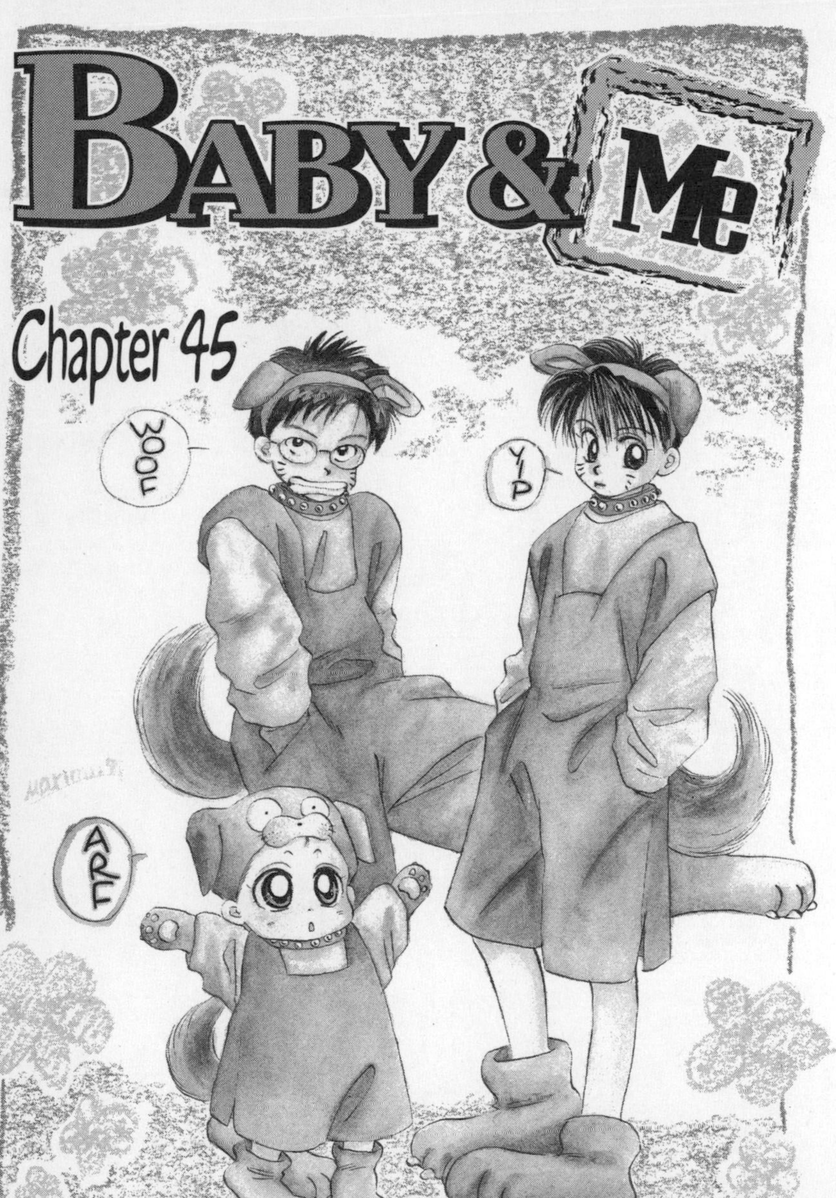
BABY & Me
Chapter 45
YIP
WOOF
ARF

It's not the right season, but they're in their bathing suits!!

A bouquet of flowers for the female co-stars!!

MODEL 1

Huh?

Tomoko Kimura, 25 years old. Blood type O

For some reason, Seiichi's wife is very popular with female readers. When she first appeared, she looked a little like Minako Tanaka, but for some reason she's gotten to be more like busty Fumie Hosokawa.

MODEL 2
Kazumi Omori, 23 years old. Blood type A
One of Takuya's dad's employees. A flashy woman with a good figure. I've never had anyone say they hate her, but then nobody's really said they like her either.

MODEL 3
Megumi Yarimizo, 12 years old. Blood type O
Room leader of the classroom next to Takuya's. She's a little strange, but popular for some reason.

MODEL 4
Shinako Fukaya, 12 years old. Blood type A
I wanted to give her an ordinary face. She's a girl who could get lost in a crowd, but doesn't.

Takuya Enoki (12 years old) The Main Character
Minoru Enoki (2 years old) The Main Character's Brother
Hitoshi Moriguchi (12 years old) Student Body President
He's a little shy.
Huh?

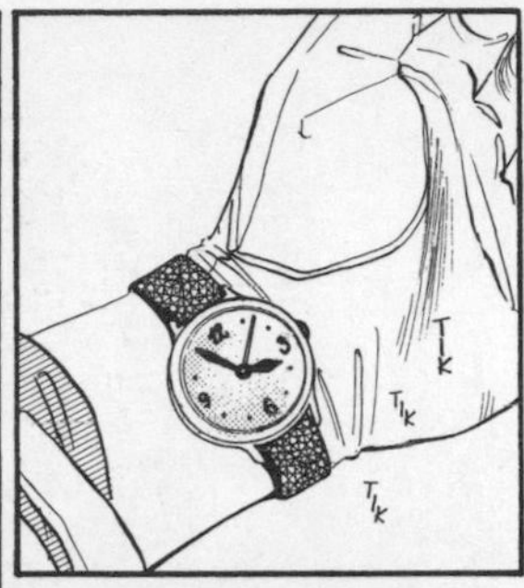

HUH?

Hand over the money

EEEK

BLAM

KA-CHAK

OKAY, EVERYBODY GET FACE-DOWN WITH YOUR HANDS ON YOUR HEAD!!

AAAAH

AAAAH

DON'T MOVE!
IF YOU PRESS THAT BUTTON, I'LL SHOOT.
KLIK!
TWITCH
!!

BLAM
KRAK
EEEEK!

HERE! PUT THE MONEY IN THIS! NOW!!
WHAP
HURRY UP OR YOU'RE DEAD.

YOU HAVE 50 SEC-ONDS!
TRY ANYTHING FUNNY AND THE GIRL GETS IT!!

CHEEP
CHEEP

BOMP BA-BA-BOMM
GOOD MORNING, IT'S 8:00 A.M. AND TIME NOW FOR THE SUNDAY MORNING NEWS.
TARO HANAYUME

ONE OF THE FOUR SUSPECTS IN THE ARMED ROBBERY OF THE SHINAGAWA BRANCH OF THE YUHI BANK..

TAKUYA, IS THE SOY SAUCE OUT THERE?

...WHICH TOOK PLACE ON THE THIRD, WAS DISCOVERED NEAR KUMANOI STATION...

NO, IT'S NOT HERE.

...AND AR-RESTED.

THE SUSPECT IS 22-YEAR-OLD KOTA YABE.

OH...

OH.

THEY CAUGHT ONE.

KLAK

WHAT?

THE BANK ROBBER...

...ON THE NEWS JUST NOW.

JUST ONE.

BUT THEY DIDN'T CATCH THE OTHERS.

Un...

HE WAS ARRESTED NEAR KUMANOI STATION.

WHAT?! THAT'S RIGHT HERE!!

YOU'D BETTER BE EXTRA CAREFUL, TAKUYA. THERE ARE STILL THREE OF THEM ON THE LOOSE.

YEAH.

NOD

DAD, WHAT ARE YOU DOING TODAY?
DO YOU WANT ME TO TAKE YOU SOME-WHERE?
ARE YOU TIRED?
I'D LIKE TO SLEEP ALL DAY...
Egg.
AT THAT POINT...

...THE BANK ROBBERY HAD NOTHING TO DO WITH OUR LITTLE WORLD.
THEN I'LL GO PLAY WITH MINORU.
MINORU, DO YOU WANT TO GO SOME-WHERE?
MOUN-TAIN.
THAT'S A LITTLE TOO FAR...
103
MORIGUCHI
...

WHO'S THIS WOMAN?
WHAT'S HER PICTURE DOING IN THIS BOOK?
CALORIES

KREEK
HITOSHI ...
HIS FATHER
AHH

YOUR MOTHER'S LEAVING FOR WORK. YOU'D BETTER SEE HER OFF.
HUH?!
HOW COME ?

WHAT?
YOUR MOTHER HAS TO WORK ON SUNDAY!
DON'T YOU THINK IT'D BE NICE TO SEE HER OFF?!

I DON'T REMEMBER GIVING BIRTH TO SUCH A CHILD!
YOU CAN'T GIVE BIRTH!
You're a man.

OH.

WHAT ARE YOU DOING WITH MY BOOK?
I HAVE TO DO SOME RESEARCH FOR HOME-WORK.
IS THIS YOUR BOOK, DAD?
YES.

YIKES!
THAT MEANS...!!

IS THIS A PICTURE OF DAD'S LOVER?!
DOOM
HUH?
WHAT ARE YOU DOING? HURRY UP.

WHAT IS IT?
YOU DON'T HAVE TO SEE ME OFF.

HAVE FUN?
AN OLD FRIEND'S COMING TO VISIT.

BUT DAD SAID...
HA HA...
HE JUST FEELS GUILTY BECAUSE HE'S GOING TO HAVE FUN TODAY AND I HAVE TO WORK.

HMM...
UH, MOM...
YES?

WHAT IF, JUST WHAT IF...
YES?
WHAT IF, UM...

THAT'S IMPOS-SIBLE.
UM... JUST TRY TO IMAGINE.
WHAT ARE YOU TALKING ABOUT?
WELL, THEN WHAT IF...

...DAD FELL IN LOVE WITH SOMEONE ELSE? WHAT WOULD YOU DO?

HMM... IF SOMETHING LIKE THAT HAPPENED...
IT'S JUST A... HYPOTHETICAL QUESTION.
BLUSH

THAT'S A STRANGE THING TO ASK.
...DAD HAD ANOTHER WOMAN'S PICTURE HIDDEN AWAY IN A BOOK? WHAT WOULD YOU DO IF YOU FOUND IT?

WHAT ?!
BUT...WHY?! AT LEAST GIVE HIM A CHANCE TO EXPLAIN!!

I'D DI-VORCE HIM!

WHY ARE YOU GETTING SO UPSET? IT'S JUST A HYPOTHETICAL QUESTION, RIGHT?
W-WELL... UM...
DON'T WORRY.
FLAP
FLAP
FUMIKO, YOUR LUNCH...
HEE HEE
I MADE YOU MIXED SUSHI.
NYAN NYAN
WHAT WOMAN WOULD BE ATTRACTED TO THAT?
TRUE.
?
WHIP
WHIP
DAD!!
TELL ME THE TRUTH!!
...
WHAT AN UNPLEASANT FACE YOU'RE MAKING!
I DON'T REMEM-BER GIVING BIRTH TO A CHILD--
YOU CAN'T GIVE BIRTH!!
DO YOU LIKE WOMEN ...
...WITH HAIR LIKE THIS?
HUH?

Author's Note: Part 1

Hello, Marimo Ragawa here.

Phew...This is my last comic book for 1994. I published four volumes this year, which was very satisfying. I sure worked hard. I was "Serious Ragawa" this year. As for my future plans, my first collection of drawings will come out at the beginning of 1995. Wheeee! Boom! Boom! But I'm sad because no one understands just how happy this makes me. Most of the drawings will be based on Baby and Me, but I plan to include some others too, so please look out for it. (I'm going to include the drawing of the guy in the center of page 189. Yes, sir.)

Oh, and please buy my 1995 Baby and Me calendar, too.

It's good to have a lot of work, but my mind and body are both exhausted.

LIKE THIS?

...

OH, I GET IT!
FWUP
...

I SUPPORT YOU NO MATTER WHAT KIND OF GIRL YOU FALL IN LOVE WITH.
SPARKLE
SPARKLE
THIS IS ABOUT YOU, NOT ME!!
SPARKLE
DON'T WORRY. I'D NEVER BE MEAN TO HER. ♡
FWUP...

OIO
POLO
WUZZ
WUZZ

HE MISUNDERSTOOD!!
YOU'VE GOT IT WRONG!
DON'T BE EMBARRASSED.
HO HO HO HO
WHIP WHIP

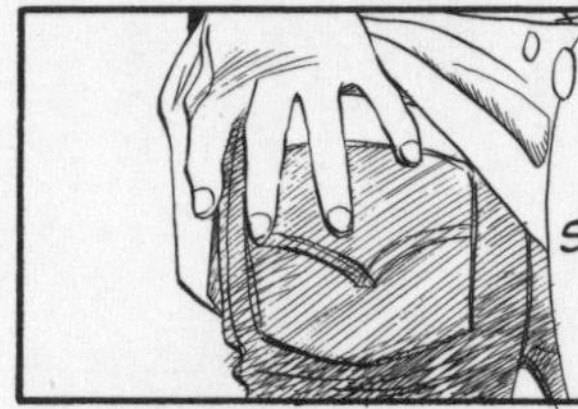
WHAT SHOULD I DO?
I FORGOT I SLIPPED THE PICTURE INTO MY POCKET...

SHOP NOVA
FWUP

MAIN SHOP STATIONARY
HEY! YOUR HANDKERCHIEF...
WUZZ
WUZZ

OH...

DAD WITH A WOMAN?
I NEVER THOUGHT OF THAT.
SIGH...
BAZAAR

THE POLICE NEED YOUR HELP
8-19
OH.
IT'S A WANTED POSTER FOR THAT GANG OF BANK ROBBERS.
WUZZ
WUZZ
HUH?
THE POLICE NEED YOUR HE

HUH? WHAT THE HECK?
RUSTLE
RUSTLE

THE HANDKERCHIEF!
IT'S GONE!!
BA-BUMP
WHERE IS IT?!
BA-BUMP

OH NO! THIS IS TERRIBLE ...
TMP
I MUST'VE DROPPED IT!!

!!

THAT KID'S GOT IT!
This ⇨

HEY, KID!
BA-BUMP

WHOA! IT'S A COP!!

SWIP :
THIS IS BAD...
HUH?

HEY, MORI-GUCHI.
HEY.

IT'S THE ONLY BIG BOOK-STORE AROUND HERE.
STARE

OH, TAKUYA.
WERE YOU IN THE BOOK-STORE?
WE WERE THERE A LITTLE WHILE AGO.

IS THIS THE FAMOUS MINORU WITH THE BROTHER COMPLEX?
FAMOUS?
UH, YEAH...
STARE..

WHAT A SOFT CHEEK.
HUH?
FOKE
AAGH!
WHUMP
PLUP..

T-TAKUYA ...
...HIS NOSE IS RUNNING ...
WHAT ?!
WHAT HAPPENED ?
I DON'T KNOW !
SNIFF

OH NO...
I DON'T HAVE ANY TISSUES.
RUSTLE
RUSTLE

ME NEITHER.
OH YEAH...
SNIFF

I FOUND THIS HAND-KERCHIEF. USE IT.
HUH? YOU FOUND IT? ARE YOU SURE IT'S OKAY?
SURE. WHO'S GONNA MISS IT?

HMM ...
WHUP

HEY ...
THERE'S SOME-THING WRITTEN ON IT.
Right 0 ③
Left 2 ②
5963194

IT'S OKAY.
Well, then...
OKAY, SAY "HMM."
HMM...
HONK

I'LL WASH IT AND TAKE IT TO THE POLICE BOX LATER.
YOU'RE A GOOD CITIZEN, TAKUYA.

BY THE WAY, WOULD YOU MIND HOLDING ON TO A PHOTOGRAPH FOR ME?
A PHOTO-GRAPH?

YEAH.
HERE IT IS.
OH... IT'S A WOMAN.

I CAN'T HAVE THIS IN MY HOUSE. IT'LL DESTROY OUR FAMILY.
WHAT?
SIGH

I WONDER...
...IF THE COP'S GONE YET...
BA-BUMP
BA-BUMP
BA-BUMP

HUH?
WAIT A MINUTE... THEY DON'T KNOW WHAT I LOOK LIKE.

I WAS HIDING FOR NOTHING.
TAP
TAP

HUH?
PARDON ME, YOUNG MAN...

CAN YOU TELL ME HOW TO GET TO THIS ADDRESS?

TA-DOOM!!

YOU OBVIOUSLY STARTLED THE YOUNG MAN.

HO HO HO HO HO

WHAT DID YOU SAY?!

MAMA...

YOU'RE BEHAVING SHAMEFULLY!! YOUR BREEDING IS SHOWING.

CHERRY!!

B-BUT

WHAT?

AH!! M-MONSTER!!

TWITCH

EEEK...

WHAT DID YOU SAY? HOW DARE YOU?!

WHAP

RANKO, YOU SHOULD LEARN TO RESPECT YOUR BETTERS!
BETTERS? YOU'D BETTER WATCH YOUR MOUTH, CHERRY...
OH YEAH? WELL, I'LL SHOW YOU--
HA HA HA HA
STOP IT THIS INSTANT!
SNEAK
SNEAK
S-SCARY... I'D BETTER GET OUTTA HERE BEFORE THEY KILL ME...
SNEAK
SNEAK
EEEK!! YOU GET ME SO MAD...
I TOLD YOU TO STOP IT, DIDN'T I?

WHAP!

103
MORIGUCHI
HMPH... WHAT'S GOING ON?

WHERE DO YOU THINK YOU'RE GOING?
EEEK!!

MEANWHILE, MR. MORIGUCHI...
SHE WAS SUPPOSED TO BE HERE AT 11:00.
THROB
THROB
DID SHE GET LOST?
HANA YUME

WOOOOOOOOOOOOO

WHAM

YOU IDIOT!
Ha... ha ha ha...
YOU DROPPED IT?! MORON!!

YOU GOT BEATEN UP BY TRANSVESTITES!! AND YOU LET THE BOY WHO FOUND IT GET AWAY!!
NOW, NOW. CALM DOWN, MITCHAN.
EEK! I'M SORRY!!
THWAK
THWAK
POOR KOTA. I CAN'T BELIEVE HE GOT CAUGHT.
WHY DID KOTA HAVE TO TRUST AKIRA WITH THE HANDKERCHIEF?!
WE'LL NEVER GET THE MONEY OUT OF THE SAFE WITHOUT THAT SECRET CODE!!

OKAY.
AKIRA?
YOU LOOKED AT THE HANDKER-CHIEF, RIGHT? CAN'T YOU REMEMBER WHAT WAS ON IT?

...

SPURT
I-IT WAS SO LONG! IT WAS TOO MUCH TROUBLE TO MEMORIZE ALL THAT.
HA HA HA

KOTA WROTE IT ALL DOWN IN CASE SOMETHING HAPPENED, AND YOU GO AND LOSE IT?! YOU'RE PATHETIC !!
THWAK
THWAK
EEEK
STOP!
...

OH, WELL ...
WE JUST HAVE TO FIND THAT KID. YOU REMEMBER WHAT HE LOOKED LIKE?
YEAH, BUT... HOW AM I GONNA GET IT BACK?
HE'LL GET SUSPICIOUS AND TELL THE COPS WHAT I LOOK LIKE!

WE'RE PEACE-LOVING PEOPLE. WE'LL JUST CONVINCE HIM TO GIVE IT BACK.
I DON'T KNOW. THAT KID WAS LOOKING AT OUR WANTED POSTER.
SHUT UP! HE'LL NEVER RECOGNIZE US FROM THOSE PICTURES.
Our faces were covered and Mitchan was wearing a disguise.

IF WORST COMES TO WORST, WE'LL USE FORCE.
WITHOUT THE MONEY, WE CAN'T LEAVE THE COUNTRY. WE HAVE TO GET THAT HANDKERCHIEF BACK. RIGHT, MITCHAN?

THAT'S RIGHT.
IF WE KILL THAT KID AND SINK HIM TO THE BOTTOM OF TOKYO BAY, WHO'S TO KNOW IT WAS US?

HA HA HA HA HA
HO HO HO HO HO

I DON'T GET IT, BUT I'LL JUST LAUGH TOO.
HYUK HYUK HYUK

WHAT ARE YOU LAUGHING ABOUT?! THIS IS SERIOUS!!
IDIOT!
EEEEK!
THWAK
THWAK

MEANWHILE, THE TRANSVESTITES...
OH, DEAR. WILL WE EVER FIND THIS PLACE?
5-CHOME? BUT WHERE'S I-CHOME?
WE CAN'T EVEN FIND A PHONE. WHAT A DISASTER.
YACK
YACK

SIGH ...
TAKUYA, YOU'RE LUCKY. YOUR DAD'S A REAL MAN.
POCARI

WELL, YOU KNOW, THE GRASS IS ALWAYS GREENER...
LET ME TELL YOU THIS. MY FATHER TALKS LIKE A WOMAN. HE EVEN WEARS MAKEUP.

YOU MEAN HE'S GUH... GUH...
I DON'T THINK HE'S GAY.

AND HE LIKES TO COOK, AND SEW, AND DO HOUSE-WORK.
I-I SEE.

ACCORDING TO MY DAD, A HOMOSEXUAL HAS THE HEART OF A WOMAN. BUT HE LOVES MY MOM, SO HE SAYS HE'S DEFINITELY GOT THE HEART OF A MAN.

I JUST WISH I COULD SEE A MORE MASCULINE SIDE OF HIM.
SOME-THING THAT SAYS, "I'M A MAN!"

DO YOU KNOW WHAT MY DAD'S DOING RIGHT NOW?
HE'S BAKING A CAKE FOR A FRIEND WHO'S COMING TO VISIT.
A CAKE !!
I JUST COULDN'T STAND TO STAY HOME.
The whole place smelled like vanilla ex-tract!!
GUETH WHAT?

MY DAD'S HOME SLEEPING.
THAT'S GREAT! THAT'S HOW A WORKING MAN SPENDS HIS WEEKENDS!!
WHAT ?!

HUH?
CAKE ITH YUMMY.
AHH...
YUM... STWAW-BEWWY...

DO YOU HAVE A GOOD HOME LIFE?
HUH? WHY?
I JUST WON-DERED.
Uh?

MORI-GUCHI ...
YOU WANNA COME PLAY AT OUR HOUSE?

WHAT?
WELL, YOU SAID YOU DIDN'T WANT TO BE AT YOUR HOUSE.
ARE YOU SURE IT'S OKAY?
NO PROB-LEM.

...

ARE YOU SURE IT'S THE BOY WITH THE GLASSES?

YEAH. HE WAS WEARING THOSE CLOTHES TOO.

...

WELL, WHAT ARE YOU WAITING FOR?
HUH?

GET HIM, YOU FOOL!
WHAM

OH... HEY...
EXCUSE ME.

DIDN'T YOU FIND A HANDKER-CHIEF?

...

I DON'T KNOW ANYTHING ABOUT IT.
OH. REALLY?

MORI-GUCHI ...
WELL, THAT HAND-KERCHIEF'S COVERED WITH SNOT.
ANYWAY, I PICKED IT UP NEAR THE STATION. WHY WOULD HE FOLLOW ME ALL THE WAY HERE?
TMP
TMP
TMP

MITCHAN, I'M BACK.
WELL? DID YOU GET IT?
HUFF
HUFF

HE DIDN'T HAVE IT.
KRAK
IDIOT! THAT'S WHAT YOU'RE ALL BREATH-LESS TO TELL ME?!

MIT-
CHAN...
WHAT IS IT,
YUSAKU?

WE'RE PEACE-LOVING PEOPLE.
BUT THAT KID NEEDS TO BE TAUGHT A LESSON!!

YUSAKU
...
BLUSH

PLEASE TEACH ME. ♡
OKAY.
DRIVE THE CAR OVER TO WHERE THE KID IS.

YUSAKU, THERE'S ANOTHER BOY AND A BABY WITH HIM.
IT'S YOUR JOB TO GET THOSE TWO OUT OF THE PICTURE.
WHAT?

H-HOW DO I DO THAT?
HEH
THAT'S FOR YOU TO FIGURE OUT.

ALL I HAVE TO DO IS GET THOSE TWO OUT OF THE WAY?
YOU HEARD ME. DON'T MAKE ME REPEAT MYSELF.

TMP
TMP
TMP
TMP
TMP
TMPTMPTMPTMP

LET'S GO PLAY!
THWAP
C'MON!! ♡
TMP TMP TMP TMP TMP TMP!!

HE'S AMAZING, BUT NOT NECESSARILY IN A GOOD WAY.
HEY?!
MORI-GUCHI!
AH!!
TMP TMP TMP TMP TMP
GULP..

YOU THERE ...
HUH?

CAN I HAVE THE HANDKERCHIEF YOU FOUND? IT BELONGS TO ME.
...

WHAT IS THIS? ARE YOU WITH THAT OTHER GUY?
WHAP
LISTEN. WE JUST WANT THE HAND-KERCHIEF, THAT'S ALL.

WHAT ARE YOU UP TO? YOU MUST'VE BEEN FOLLOWING ME EVER SINCE I PICKED IT UP NEAR THE STATION!
C'MON, KID! IT'S IMPORTANT TO ME!! IT WAS MY FATHER'S.
So you do have it.

BUT I DON'T HAVE IT.
WHAT?! WHAT DID YOU DO WITH IT?!

MY FRIEND WHO YOUR FRIEND RAN OFF WITH HAS IT...
WH-WHAT?
AKIRA!!

WHAT ARE YOU DOING, YUSAKU?!
NEVER MIND THAT. GO GET THE OTHER KID.

OH!
Huh?

PLONK
GIVE THAT WOMAN A BEAUTY MARK...
PLONK
...AND PUT A WIG LIKE THIS ON HER...

SHE'S THE FEMALE BANK ROBBER!!
TWITCH

...
THAT'S IT!
I'M GOING AFTER TAKUYA AND MINORU!!
TMP
TMP
TMP

WHAP
HUH?

YOU'RE NOT TOO BRIGHT, HUH?
TUK

YOU KNOW WHAT THIS IS, DON'T YOU?
GET IN THE CAR.
17 AUSTRIA

LOOK...
YOU CAN'T SCARE ME WITH THAT TOY.
WHAT?

MY MOTHER'S A COP!! (ACTUALLY, SHE'S IN THE TRAFFIC DEPARTMENT.)
WHAT ?
I'LL FORGET ABOUT THIS IF YOU LET ME GO RIGHT NOW!!
IT'S TOO LATE FOR THAT NOW!!
AARGH!
THWAK
GET IN THERE !!
MIT-CHAN, FIND AKIRA!
VROOOM
UNH...
WH-WHAT IS THIS?
WAIT ...
...A MINUTE !!
SIGH ...

I'M SO BORED...
I'M TIRED OF READING...
MY GUEST NEVER SHOWED UP...
...AND HITOSHI HASN'T COME HOME...
FWUMP!

HITOSHI ...
...

HMM ...
A WOMAN WITH HAIR LIKE THIS...

WHY DID HE ASK ME THAT?
I THINK HE WAS READING A BOOK BEFORE THAT...

HUH? JUST A MINUTE ...
WHAT BOOK WAS HE LOOKING AT THIS MORNING? WASN'T IT THE CALORIE BOOK?
WHUP

THE CALORIE BOOK...
THE PICTURE!!

IT'S NO USE!
WE'VE LOOKED EVERYWHERE, AND THERE'S NO I-CHOME.

CHERRY, RANKO, YOU'RE LOOKING SLOPPY. YOUR BREEDING IS SHOWING.
HUFF
HUFF
MAMA, YOUR KIMONO'S FLAPPING OPEN.
I WONDER WHY WE CAN'T FIND ANY PUBLIC PHONES...
WE'LL HAVE TO ASK SOMEONE.
FWUP
FWUP

OH, LOOK. THERE'S SOME-ONE THERE.

YOU'RE RIGHT.
OH, DEAR.

HEY, THAT BOY IN THE CAP. ISN'T THAT THE RUDE BOY WE MET BY THE STATION?
WHAT A COINCI-DENCE.
THEN YOU HAVE NO BUSINESS WITH US, RIGHT?
THAT'S RIGHT. I'M SORRY. I GUESS I GOT THE WRONG GUY.

AKIRA ...
OH, YUSAKU...
GET IN!!
CHUNK
HUH? OKAY.

DID YOU GET THE HANDKER-CHIEF?
NEVER MIND. JUST GET IN!!

Chapter 45 / The End

Chapter 46

BABY & ME

NOW HAND OVER THAT HANDKERCHIEF NICE AND PEACEFULLY.

THIS SAFE IS VERY STRONG, YOU SEE...
...AND THE SECRET CODE IS THE FASTEST WAY TO OPEN IT.
BUT KOTA WAS THE ONLY ONE WHO KNEW THE CODE, AND HE GOT ARRESTED.

DON'T BE AFRAID.
IF YOU GIVE US THE HANDKERCHIEF WITHOUT A STRUGGLE, WE'LL LET YOU GO.
NOW WHERE IS IT?
RUSTLE

!!

GOT IT!! ♡
TOOOT
BOOM
BOOM

DARN IT...
YOU GUYS WON'T GET AWAY WITH THIS!!

YOU'RE A MOUTHY BRAT, AREN'T YOU?
OH!!
MORI-GUCHI!
TOMP
UGH!!

OH. THAT'S BECAUSE HE BLEW HIS NOSE ON IT.
Minoru did.
YUCK
!!

HUH? IT'S STUCK TOGETHER.
KREK
KREK
IT'S CRACK-LING.

I...I CAN'T OPEN IT. IT'S TOO GROSS.
PLEASE ...
AKIRA, GO WASH IT OUT.
WHO, ME?

HELLO, MORIGUCHI RESIDENCE ...

IT'S ME... MAMA.
HIROSHI
SMAK
MAMA? WHERE ARE YOU? I WAS WORRIED SICK ABOUT YOU.
CHERRY AND RANKO ARE WITH ME HERE, BUT WE'RE NOT SURE WHERE WE ARE.

WE'RE NEXT TO A RUN-DOWN BUILDING.
IS IT, BY ANY CHANCE, A FIVE-STORY BUILDING SUR-ROUNDED BY A WALL?
THAT'S RIGHT.

OH, DEAR. YOU'VE GONE IN THE COMPLETE OPPOSITE DIRECTION.
JUST WAIT THERE. I'LL COME AND GET YOU.
PLEASE HURRY!

I CAN'T BELIEVE THEY COULD GET SO LOST.
THEY'RE WAY OUT ON THE EDGE OF TOWN.
But if I don't go get them, who knows where they'll end up?
KLAK

OH!

HEY! WHAT IS IT, AKIRA?
YUSAKU... THIS...THIS...
SHAKE
SHAKE

L-LOOKS LIKE...HE USED A WATER-BASED MARKER!
HA HA... HA HA HA...
THE CODE! IT'S GONE!!

!!
WHAM

WH-WHAT'S THE MATTER? YOU'RE SO PALE!
HEY, YOU TWO!! DID YOU SEE WHAT WAS ON THAT HANDKER-CHIEF?!

WHAT? YOU MEAN THOSE NUM-BERS?
YOU DID SAY THERE WAS SOMETHING WRITTEN ON IT, DIDN'T YOU?
SO YOU DID SEE IT!

I DID, BUT ONLY FOR A SECOND.
I DON'T REMEMBER WHAT WAS WRITTEN ON IT.
WHAT?

SHUP
THEN I'LL...
...HELP YOU REMEMBER.

WHAT HAP-PENED?
LOOK.
YIKES.

HEY, TAKE THOSE GUYS TO THE OTHER ROOM.
BWAAAAH
MINORU! MORI-GUCHI!
BWAZA !!
HUH?! HEY, TAKUYA!!

TO START OFF...
...WHY DON'T YOU TELL ME EVERY-THING YOU REMEM-BER?

KLAK
KLAK
KLAK

BWAAAH
LET GO!
WHAM
NOW THEN...
...

HUH ?!
CHAK
THAT'S IT.
TELL ME.
HUH?
BLAM
!!
KRAK
AH ...
RIGHT... 0...3...
L-LEFT... 2...2...
THEN, UM...

WELL?
WHAT ABOUT THE REST?

THE REST...
...WERE...

THERE WERE...

...SEVEN NUMBERS, I THINK.

MIT-CHAN...
THAT WAS A GUNSHOT.
HEY, YOU!
WHAT?
BWAZA!!

AH! AGAIN!
I WON'T LET YOU GET AWAY WITH THIS!!
BLAM
SOB

...
IF ANYTHING HAPPENS TO MY FRIEND...
...I'LL KILL YOU ALL!!

Author's Note: Part 2

As for the story of the soup in Baby and Me volume 8, depending on the dictionary you use, it seems there are two ways of writing *omiotsuke*. Sorry for blaming you, teachers. Now let's all put this behind us. Please.

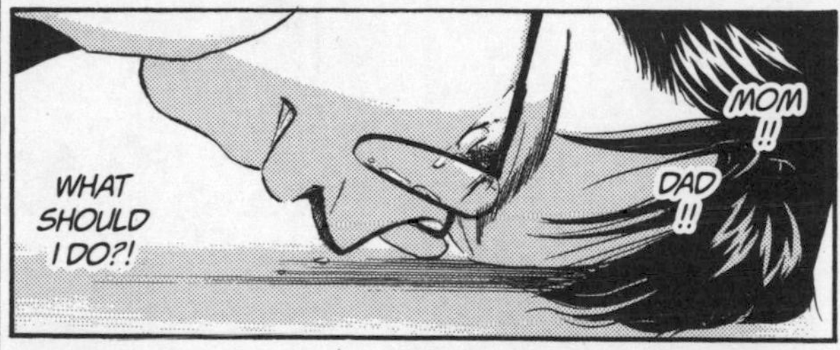

VROOM...

OH...
PULL OVER.
HUH?

DEAR ...

OH, FUMIKO ...
WHERE ARE YOU GOING?
TO GET MY FRIEND WHO WAS COMING TO VISIT.

THEN WE CAN TAKE YOU.
NO, THAT'S OKAY. YOU'RE ON THE JOB.
HUH? WHAT?! THAT'S STRAIGHT-AS-AN-ARROW MORIGUCHI'S HUSBAND?!

IT'S OKAY, RIGHT?
She won't take no for an answer.
OH... SURE.
SMILE

MEANWHILE, THE TRANSVESTITES...
I'M SO HUNGRY.
THESE COOKIES ARE PRETTY GOOD.
THOSE COOKIES WERE FOR HIM.
MUNCH
MUNCH
KRUNCH
KRUNCH

WELL?
DO YOU RE-MEM-BER NOW?
B-BUT ...
I-I ONLY CAUGHT A GLIMPSE OF IT.
IF YOU DON'T REMEMBER...
...YOUR FRIEND AND THAT SHRIMP ARE GONNA GET IT.
I-I DON'T KNOW ...
THINK, TAKUYA, THINK!
CHAK
HEY!
WHAM
YUSAKU, WHAT ARE YOU DOING?!

I'M HELPING THE BOY REMEMBER.

ANYTHING'S POSSIBLE... WITH THE RIGHT PERSUASION.
BUT WHAT IF HE REALLY CAN'T REMEMBER?

YOU'RE NOT CHICKENING OUT, ARE YOU?
WE ALL AGREED WE'D KILL THEM, DIDN'T WE?

UM...
NO MATTER HOW MUCH YOU THREATEN HIM, HE CAN'T REMEMBER SOMETHING THAT HE DOESN'T KNOW.
HUH?

THEN...WE COULD TRY DIFFERENT SETS OF NUMBERS.
DO YOU REALIZE HOW MANY POSSIBLE COMBINATIONS OF NUMBERS THERE ARE? WE DON'T EVEN KNOW THE NUMBER OF DIGITS.

I FEEL SORRY FOR HIM!! YOU DON'T HAVE TO DO THIS! OH!
I KNOW!! LET'S BLOW THE SAFE!!
YOU IDIOT!
THE PAPER MONEY INSIDE WOULD GET BLOWN TO BITS.

THEN... THEN...
SHUT UP!

YUSAKU...

WE NEED THAT MONEY!!

WE'RE GONNA LEAVE THE COUNTRY AND START A NEW LIFE, RIGHT?

DO YOU WANNA KEEP LIVING LIKE THIS FOREVER?!

YOU'D BETTER NOT BE MESSING WITH ME.
YOU SURE?
THAT'S WHAT IT WAS.
5963194.
I THINK THAT WAS IT.

HUH?
THAT'S IT?

5963194!!

HEH...
GOOD JOB. YOU'RE SMARTER THAN AKIRA.

IT JUST WASN'T YOUR LUCKY DAY, THAT'S ALL.
HUH?
YUSAKU !!
GULP!

WHUP

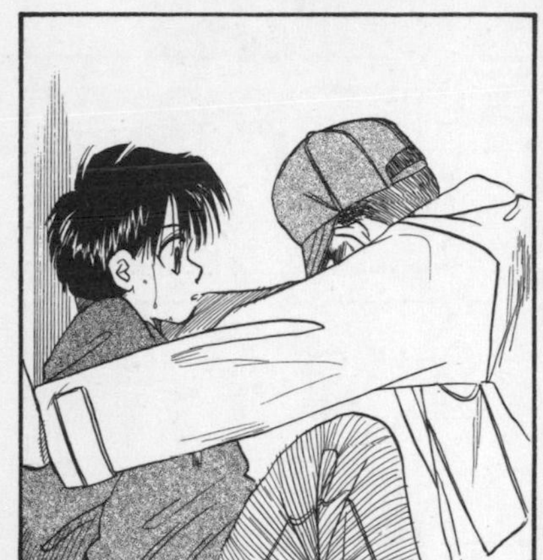
...?

HUH?

KLAK...

WHAT'S WRONG, AKIRA?
YUSAKU ...

DID YOU REALLY THINK I'D SHOOT HIM NOW?

NO REASON ...
...TO KILL HIM YET.

YOU'RE RIGHT.
I CAN KILL HIM ANY-TIME.
A LITTLE WHILE WON'T MATTER.

WOOSH

BWAZA!
BUMP...
TAKUYA!

YOU'RE GOOD BOYS...
...SO KEEP QUIET, OKAY?

WHAM
CHAK
ARE YOU ALL RIGHT, TAKUYA?
Y-YEAH.
AH! BWAZA!

HEY! MINORU, YOUR HANDS AREN'T TIED.
WAH...
SOB SOB

I UNTIED HIM WITH MY TEETH.
GOOD THING SHE DIDN'T NOTICE.
This
TAKUYA...

WE MIGHT BE ABLE TO GET OUT THROUGH THAT VENT.
WHAT? BUT IT'S TOO SMALL.

MINORU COULD DO IT.
!!
M-MINORU?
HE'LL HAVE TO GO FOR HELP.

...

MINO-RU...
UH...

IT'S OKAY.
YOU CAN DO IT, CAN'T YOU?

YETH.
DOOM

YOU HAVE THAT PICTURE I GAVE YOU, RIGHT?
YEAH. JUST A MINUTE, IT'S IN MY BACK POCKET.
RUSTLE
RUSTLE

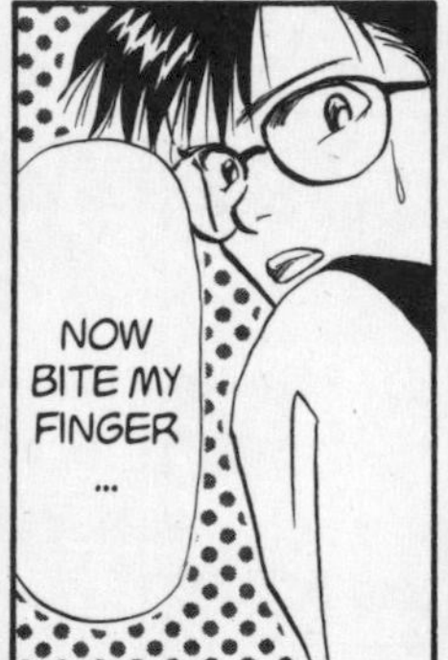
NOW BITE MY FINGER ...

HUH?
I NEED SOME BLOOD. YOU DON'T HAVE ANYTHING TO WRITE WITH, DO YOU?

I-IT'S GONNA HURT.
THAT'S OKAY.
HURRY UP.

SCARY.
CHONK

OUCH ...
IS IT BLEEDING?
Y-YES.

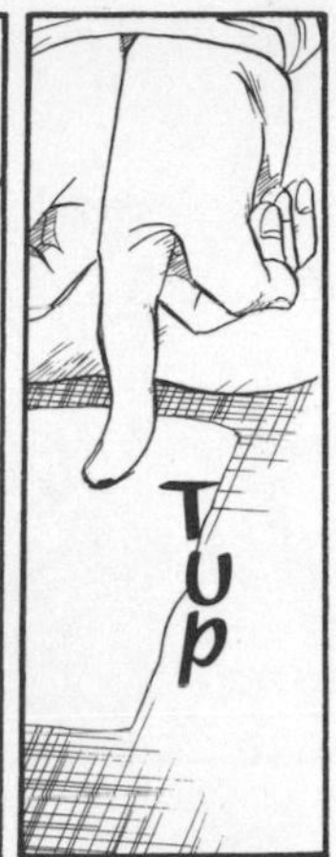
TUP

HOLD IT DOWN.
DOES IT HURT?
YEAH.
SWFF
SWFF

NOW ...
HMPH

CHOMP

POP
UNGH...
GEEZ, MORIGUCHI!

MINORU, DO WHAT I TOLD YOU.
OGAY.
UGH... OUCH.

KOFF KOFF
MINORU, GRAB HOLD OF ME.
OGAY.

...

BE STRONG, MINORU!
OGAY !!
TUP
TUP

RIGHT, ZERO THREE.
LEFT, TWENTY-TWO.

ZERO AND THREE ?
NO, IT PROBABLY MEANS ZERO THREE TIMES.
KLIK
KLIK

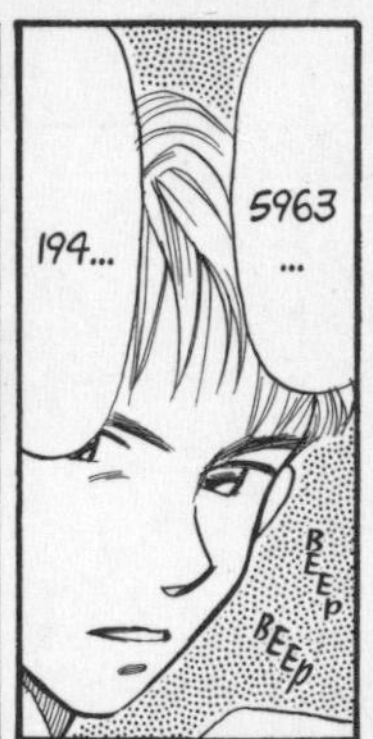
5963 ...
194...
BEEP
BEEP

CHAK
IT'S OPENING!!

WE DID IT!

WHAT?

KOTA DOUBLE-CROSSED US!!

HUH?
WHAT?
KOTA
...

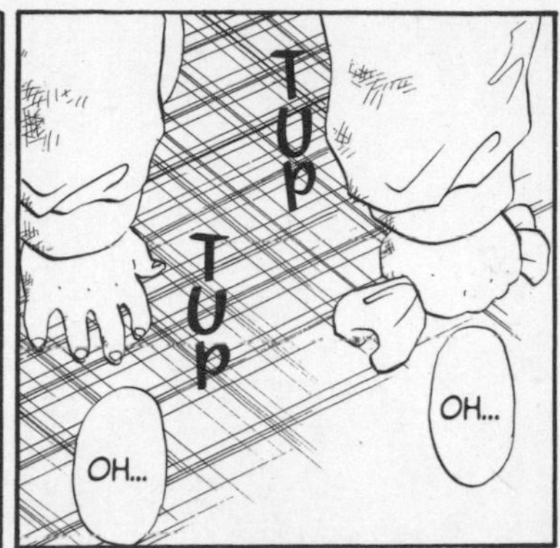
TUP
TUP
OH...
OH...

WAAH... BWAZA... DADDY...
MINOWU SCAWED ...
TUP
TUP

MI-NORU ...
YOU CAN DO IT, CAN'T YOU?
DUOOM
YETH.

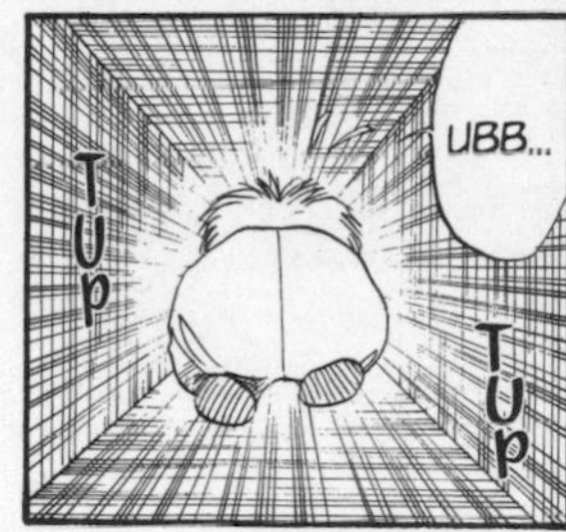
UBB...
TUP
TUP

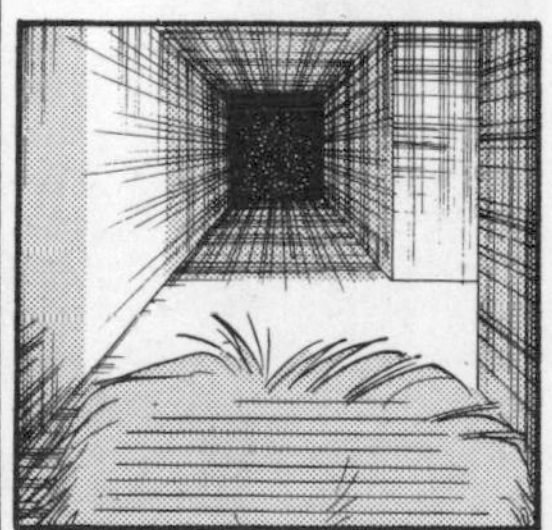

SIGH...

I'M TIRED OF WAITING, AREN'T YOU?

WHAT IS IT?!

AH!

HA HA... MY KNEES GAVE WAY...

WAAAAH

OH! THAT SOUNDS LIKE A BABY CRYING!

YOU TAKE A LOOK.

NO!! I'M SCARED!

AH!

YOU'LL BE ALL RIGHT.

WHAP

OF THE THREE OF US, I'M THE MOST FRAGILE.
SOB
IF IT COMES TO IT, WE'LL GATHER UP YOUR BONES.

WHAP

WHO IS IT?
KAKLANK
WHAT STRENGTH!

OH!

A CHILD.
AH...
Scared

MAMA, CHERRY...
IT'S A CHILD!!
WHAT?!
WHAT?!
TMP TMP TMP TMP

VEEN

BLUB
BLUB
BLUB
...

GWAAAH
HE'P! MONS'ERS!
WHAT AN ANNOYING CHILD...

HOW CUTE!♡

HUH?
THERE'S SOMETHING IN HIS HAND.

SKREECH

THANKS FOR WAITING. I'M SORRY IT TOOK SO LONG.
CHUNK

HUH?
WHICH OF YOU GAVE BIRTH TO HIM?

WE CAN'T GIVE BIRTH.

OH, FUMIKO ...
IT'S GOOD TO SEE YOU AGAIN. MY HUSBAND'S VERY GRATEFUL TO YOU.
OH, MY...
HO HO HO
BOW

NEVER MIND THAT. HIROSHI, SOMETHING TERRIBLE HAS HAPPENED.

WHAT? THESE ARE MRS. MORI-GUCHI'S FRIENDS?
THIS CHILD JUST CAME OUT OF THAT BUILDING. LOOK AT THE PICTURE HE HAD IN HIS HAND!!

PIC-TURE?
THIS ONE. LOOK.
ISN'T THIS A PICTURE OF YOUR... YOU-KNOW-WHAT?
HUH?

DOOM
WHAT?
WHAT'S THIS PICTURE DOING HERE?!

WHAT IS IT?
OH NO!! IT'S NOTHING...
WHAP

HUH?
THIS IS THE PICTURE THAT HITOSHI TOOK?

IF THIS IS HERE, THEN... WHERE'S HITOSHI?
LOOK ON THE BACK.

WHAT? THE BACK?
OH!
FWIP

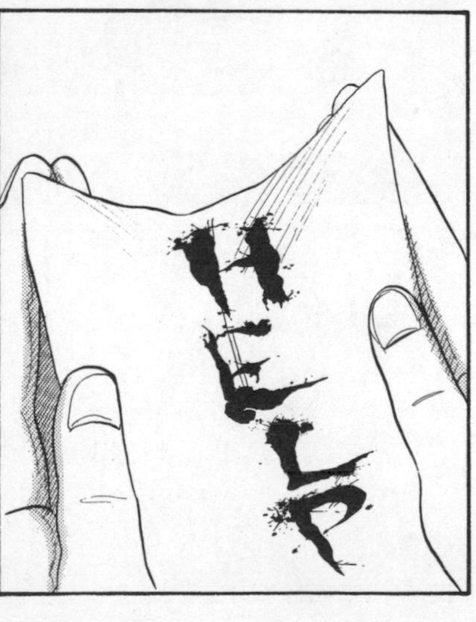
HELP

IT'S WRITTEN IN BLOOD!
HITOSHI!!

OH MY GOODNESS! I THINK I SAW THIS LITTLE BOY GETTING INTO A CAR.
Now she remem-bers?
Better late than never.
ANYONE ELSE? WERE THERE OTHER CHIL-DREN?

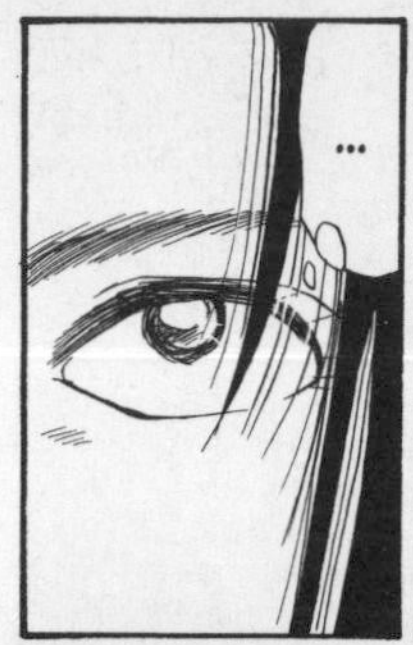
...

YES! THERE WAS A HANDSOME BOY AND, I COULDN'T SEE TOO CLEARLY, BUT I THINK THERE WAS ANOTHER ONE IN THE CAR.
DIDN'T YOU THREE THINK THERE WAS SOMETHING STRANGE ABOUT THAT?!
What?
WHAK

THEY'VE BEEN KID-NAPPED.

NOW, FUMIKO, YOU'RE JUMPING TO CONCLU-SIONS.
I'M A POLICE OFFICER !!

THIS IS HARD TO SAY, BUT...
WHAT IS IT?

HITOSHI WAS ONE OF THE BOYS WHO WAS KIDNAPPED.

...

WHUMP
FUMIKO!!
She's a mother, after all.

I WONDER IF MINORU MADE IT OUT OKAY?
WE CAN ONLY HOPE HE DID.

YEAH.
HE'S OKAY.
HE'S GOT TO BE OKAY!!

WHAM

DARN!

I NEVER THOUGHT KOTA WOULD DOUBLE-CROSS US!!

Y-YUSAKU...

I GUESS WE SHOULDN'T HAVE BEEN SO TRUSTING.

YUSAKU, WHAT'RE WE GONNA DO WITH THOSE KIDS?

...

WE DON'T EVEN HAVE THE MONEY, SO...

YOU KNOW WHAT WE HAVE TO DO.

WE MAY NOT HAVE THE MONEY, BUT WE DID ROB THE BANK. AND THEY'VE SEEN OUR FACES.

WE HAVE NO CHOICE. WE HAVE TO KILL THEM.

Chapter 46 / The End

Chapter 47

BABY & ME

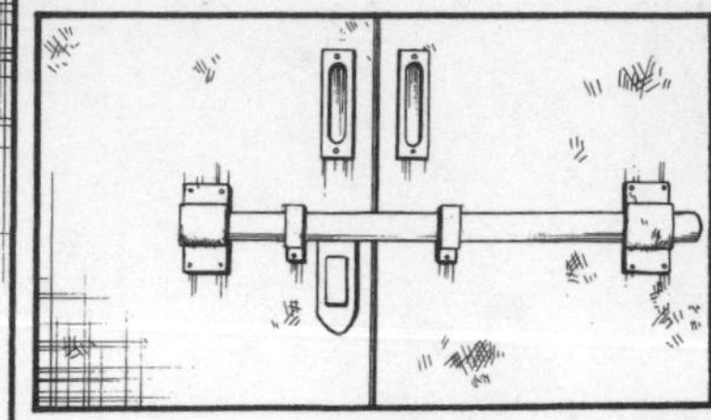

CHAK
KLANG...

...

...?
HEY... WHERE'S THE SHRIMP?
OH.
YUSAKU, LOOK THERE.

THE AIR VENT.
FWOOO

YOU PUNKS ...
YOU THINK YOU'RE PRETTY SMART, DON'T YOU?

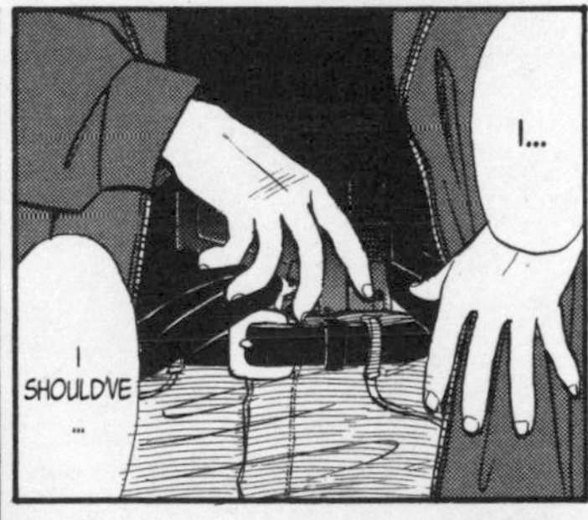
I...
I SHOULD'VE ...

I UNDER-ESTI-MATED ...
CHAK
...YOU TWO.

...KILLED YOU SOONER.

YU-SAKU ...
WAIT A MINUTE.

WHAT, MITCHAN?
LET'S USE OUR HEADS.

IF THAT LITTLE ONE GOT AWAY, WE HAVE TO GET OUT OF HERE AS SOON AS POSSIBLE.

AND WE'RE GOING TO NEED HOSTAGES. IF THEY CORNER US, THEY'RE OUR ONLY CHANCE.

...

GOOD THINK-ING.
PHEW...
SWUFF...
THANK GOOD-NESS...

COME ON.
GET UP!!
TUG
GET UP.
C'MON.

MINORU!!
HURRY!! SOMEBODY, PLEASE HURRY!!

!!

A PATROL CAR?!
WE'RE IN TROUBLE!!
WHAT ?!
THE COPS ARE OUTSIDE!!

LET'S GO OUT THE BACK!!
YOU'RE GONNA GET CAUGHT ANYWAY!! WHY DON'T YOU GIVE YOURSELVES UP?!
!!

SHUT UP, YOU!
WHAK

M-MORIGUCHI, ARE YOU ALL RIGHT?
OW...

SHHH ...

!!
KLAK KLAK KLAK

SOMEBODY HELP!!
HUH?
WHAT'S WRONG, HIROSHI?
DIDN'T YOU HEAR THAT?
HUH?
I DON'T HEAR ANYTHING.

KOFF

TWITCH
WHAT THE ...?

HIS EYES ...
THEY REMIND ME OF KOTA'S.
OH! WHAT SHOULD WE DO?

THERE ARE STAIRS GOING UP AND STAIRS GOING DOWN.
SHALL WE SPLIT UP?

ALL RIGHT, THAT'S WHAT WE'LL DO!!

ALL OF YOU GO UP.
I'LL TAKE THE BASE-MENT.
BUT YOU'LL BE ALONE...
I HAVE A GUN!!

I'M A POLICE OFFICER!!
BESIDES, MY JUNIOR OFFICER IS CALLING FOR BACKUP, SO I'LL BE FINE!!
KRK

THERE'S A GROUP OF SUSPECTED KIDNAPPERS IN THE BUILDING.

HURRY!
PLEASE COME QUICKLY.
OKAY!! JUST CALM DOWN.
KRAK

WAAAAH
WAAAAH
BWAZAAA!!
HUH? WHAT? I CAN'T HEAR YOU.
WHAT? I CAN'T HEAR A WORD YOU'RE SAYING!

HUFF
KLAK
HUFF
KLAK
KLAK
HUFF

THE HIGHER WE GO...
...THE HARDER IT'LL BE TO ESCAPE.

...
SHE'S RIGHT. YUSAKU, WHAT'LL WE DO?

!!
SHUT UP, WILL YOU?! STOP ASKING ME WHAT TO DO!!
THAT'S WHY PEOPLE ALWAYS THINK YOU'RE A FOOL!!
YOU'RE DEAD WEIGHT!!

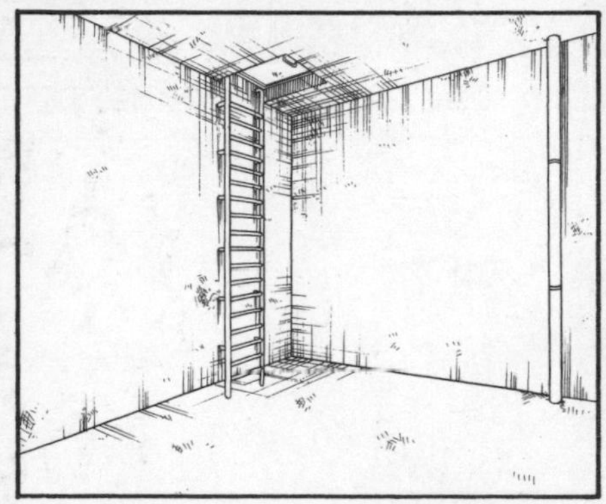

STAY HERE.
HUH? WHAT ABOUT YOU, YUSAKU?
I'LL GO HAVE A LOOK AROUND.

AKIRA ...

!!
THUMP

NOW LISTEN, I WANT YOU TO KEEP AN EYE ON THOSE KIDS.
YOU'RE IN CHARGE.
WHUP
A... ALL RIGHT.
AKIRA...
WH-WHAT IS IT, MIT-CHAN?
DON'T LET IT GET TO YOU.
YUSAKU'S UPSET ABOUT KOTA DOUBLE-CROSSING US.

?
...

I'LL TELL YOU THIS BECAUSE YOU SEEM TO BE A GOOD PERSON.
YOU'RE WALKING DEEPER AND DEEPER INTO QUICK-SAND.

WHY DON'T YOU SURREN-DER?
IF YOU KILL US, THERE'LL BE NO TURNING BACK.

THOSE TWO REALIZE THAT.
THEY DON'T LIKE THIS SITUATION ANY MORE THAN YOU DO.
BUT I...I CAN'T BETRAY THEM.
I DON'T WANT TO LOSE THEM.
BUT WHY? THEY'RE AWFUL PEOPLE.
THEY'RE NOT AWFUL.
WE'VE BEEN FRIENDS SINCE OUR DAYS IN THE ORPHANAGE.
AS YOU CAN PROBABLY TELL, I'M NOT ALL THAT SMART.
PEOPLE ALWAYS MAKE FUN OF ME.
I HAVE TROUBLE TALKING TO PEOPLE.
I DON'T KNOW WHAT YOU'RE SAYING. CAN'T YOU SPEAK UP?
IT'S YOUR FAULT WE DIDN'T MAKE OUR QUOTA.
YOU IDIOT.
YOU CAN JUST STAY HERE TILL YOU FINISH THE WORK.
AKIRA ...
OVER HERE.
IS YOUR JOB TOUGH?
MITCHAN, YOU'RE SO DIFFERENT NOW.
HA
HA

...

MORI-GUCHI ...
HUH?
WE'RE GOING TO BE ALL RIGHT.
WHY DO YOU SAY THAT?

WHEN HE THREATENED ME INTO REMEMBERING THE CODE FOR THE SAFE...
...I WAS SCARED. I THOUGHT HE WAS REALLY GOING TO SHOOT ME.

HE SAYS HE'LL KILL US, BUT...
...HE SEEMS TO BE STRETCHING THINGS OUT, TRYING TO AVOID IT.
I DON'T THINK HE REALLY WANTS TO KILL US.

TA-KUYA, YOU...
HUH?
YOU'RE REALLY NOT WORRIED, HUH?
WHAT?

WHEN I THOUGHT I WAS GOING TO DIE, I KEPT THINKING ABOUT ALL THE THINGS I WANTED TO DO.
LIKE WHAT?
ALL SORTS OF THINGS...

AKIHIRO'S SUPER FAMICOM GAME THAT I NEED TO RETURN...
AND MY STUDENT COUNCIL RESPONSIBILITIES...
AND HOW I SHOULD'VE TALKED TO MY MOM AND DAD MORE.

I WISH I'D PLAYED WITH MINORU'S CHEEKS MORE.
WHY? HIS NOSE WOULD JUST RUN AGAIN.
AND ...
...I WISH I'D ASKED MY DAD WHO THE WOMAN IN THE PICTURE WAS.
THAT'S YOUR DAD'S PICTURE?
MAYBE SHE'S HIS LOVER. I SHOULD'VE TOLD MY MOM ABOUT IT.

HEH
IF WE GET OUT OF THIS ALIVE, YOU CAN TELL HER.
YEAH. I CAN'T WAIT TO TELL HER.
HEH HEH HEH HEH
WHY ARE YOU SMILING?
HUH? WELL...

I...
I JUST LIKE LISTENING TO YOU TALK.
KLAK
KLAK
MONEY'S BEEN DISAP-PEARING FROM THE SHOP.
KLAK

SO...
...I SEARCHED YOUR BELONG-INGS.

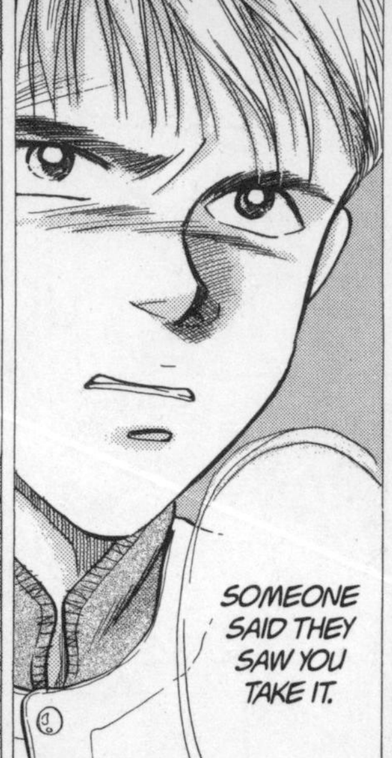
SOMEONE SAID THEY SAW YOU TAKE IT.

IT MAKES ME SO MAD. WHENEVER THERE'S TROUBLE AT THE SHOP, THEY ALWAYS SUSPECT ME.
MICHINOKU
GRILLED SMELT
ICED TOFU

I NEVER TOOK ANY MONEY FROM THAT SHOP.
IT CAN'T BE HELPED.

WE HAVE A RECORD.
IT'S ONLY NATURAL FOR THEM TO SUSPECT US.
KOTA...

LOOK, WE'RE OUT OF REFORM SCHOOL, NOW...
...AND WE'VE DECIDED TO GO STRAIGHT.

I BELIEVE IN YOU.
LET'S NOT GIVE UP.
KLUNK..

BUT I CAN'T STAND IT...
I'VE BEEN TRYING TO STRAIGHTEN MYSELF OUT.

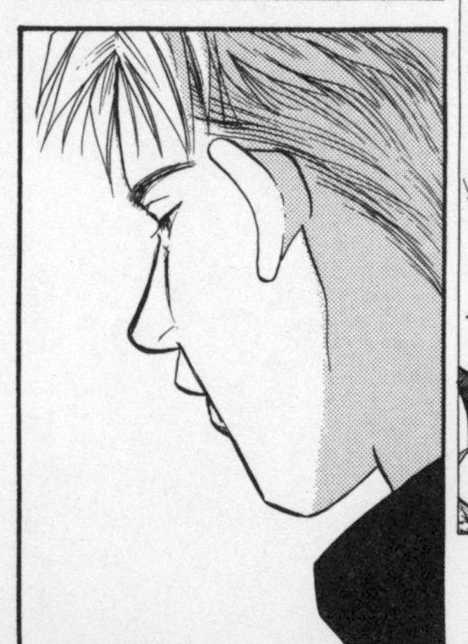

KOTA...
DID...
DID YOU REALLY BELIEVE IN ME?!
NO ONE HERE EITHER.
OH.
A SAFE.
KLAK
WHAT'S IT DOING HERE?
KLAK
IT'S PRETTY BANGED UP.
LOOKS LIKE SOMEONE TRIED TO FORCE IT OPEN.
SH-SH-SHELL CASINGS !!
OH NO! WHAT HAP-PENED?!
SNAP

BULLET HOLES IN THE WALL...

OH...
WHUMP

OH NO!!

OH, DEAR. THERE'S NO ONE HERE EITHER.
MAYBE THEY'RE UP THERE.

HMPH. THEY SHOULD TEAR DOWN ROTTEN BUILDINGS LIKE THIS.
!!

YOU KNOW, THEY SAY THAT FOOLS AND BRAVE PEOPLE LIKE HIGH PLACES.
As if!

HOW MANY OF THEM ARE THERE?
SOUNDS LIKE THEY'RE ALL WOMEN.
CHAK

MAYBE WE CAN USE THE EMERGENCY EXIT.

Author's Note: Part 3

I did this bank robbery story because I wanted to go at Baby and Me from a different angle. It was a lot of fun to draw, even though it was a pain drawing so many characters.

Yusaku was pretty popular, but some people didn't like his name. 66

Chapter 46 Anecdote

Originally, I'd intended for there to be money in the safe, but I was really short on pages, so I expanded a two-part story to three parts. Then I decided that there couldn't be money in the safe if I was going to keep the story going for another chapter. So the money had to go.

!!

THERE HE IS!!

H- HOLD ON!!
I'VE THROWN OUT MY BACK!
MAMA...
TMP TMP TMP TMP
HI-TOSHI!!
I'M COMING!!
BLAM
!!

YUSAKU, WHAT IS IT? I HEARD A SHOT.
THE COPS GOT US SUR-ROUNDED.
AND THERE'S SOME WEIRD PEOPLE COMING THIS WAY.

KNOW WHAT?

THE ROOF ...

CAW COME...
...AN' DEY TIE MY HANDS!
HIC
HIC

BWAZA BITED HIM'S FINGEW.
HIC
HIC
HMM... GREAT...
I CAN'T UNDER-STAND A WORD HE'S SAYING!!
AND YOUR NAME IS MINOWU? IS THAT RIGHT?

I- INSPECTOR, UP THERE!!

THEY'RE ON THE ROOF!
WAAH
WAAH
WAAH

YUSAKU...

WOOOOOO

NOW...

...WHAT'LL WE DO?

HUH?

WHAT DO YOU THINK?

W-WELL...

I THINK WE'RE FINISHED.

WANNA END IT ALL?
YOU COULD JUMP.

NOBODY CARES IF WE LIVE OR DIE.

!!
...
THERE ISN'T ANYTHING FOR US ANYWAY.

WHAP

YOU !!
STOP FEELING SORRY FOR YOURSELF!!
WHUMP

DA...

DAD!!
NOW LISTEN, YOU! I'LL SEE THAT YOU PAY FOR WHAT YOU'VE DONE!!

I DON'T KNOW WHAT YOUR PROBLEM IS, BUT YOU'RE BREAKING YOUR PARENTS' HEARTS!

...
WE'RE ORPHANS.

POOR THINGS ...
SO THAT'S WHY THEY BECAME DELINQUENTS. LET'S LET THEM GO.
Little Orphan Bees...
PLUP..
WHAT'S WRONG WITH YOU?!

YIKES! IT'S THOSE TRANSVES-TITES!!
TWITCH
WHAT DID YOU SAY?!
GET HIM!
THWAK
EEEK
THWAK
JUST LET THE KIDS GO!
OH!
KLAK..

THIS IS PERFECT. IF YOU DON'T WANT ME TO KILL YOUR KID...
...GO DOWN AND GIVE THE COPS A MESSAGE !!

TELL THEM I WANT A HELI-COPTER.
...

TMP

WHY, YOU...
SWAK
TAKUYA !!

AH!
!!
WHAM

CHOMP
YOUCH!

LOUSY BRAT...
WHAK
UGH ...

FREEZE!!
MOVE AND I'LL KILL YOU!!
CHAK

THE ONE ...
THE ONE ...

THE ONE WHO'S GONNA DIE IS YOU!!
!!
THIS IS FOR KIDNAPPING THESE SWEET CHILDREN!!
DIVINE PUNISH-MENT!
WHAM
!!
FWUMP

HMPH!!

H-HIROSHI SNAPPED...
I HAVEN'T SEEN THAT FOR A WHILE...
YAY

CHAK
DON'T MOVE.

IF YOU MOVE...
...I'LL KILL YOU.

MITCHAN...
YUSAKU, AKIRA, GET OVER HERE QUICK.

UM, SORRY TO INTERRUPT YOU, BUT...
WHAT DO YOU WANT, FREAK?
I'M BUSY HERE!!

FREAK?
AREN'T YOU MICHIO WHO WORKS DOWN ON 2-CHOME? ARE THOSE BREASTS REAL?
WHAT ?!
STUNNED
OH, MY. IT IS YOU.
I THOUGHT YOU WERE GAY, BUT YOU'RE A TRANSVESTITE TOO?
How cute.

NO. DON'T COME NEAR ME.
YOU SHOULDN'T DO THINGS LIKE THIS.
HUH?

SHE'S A MAN?!

AK AK AK
AK AK AK AK
OOOH !!
STOP!!
WHAT ARE YOU DOING, MICHIO?

I...
DON'T TALK TO ME LIKE WE'RE OLD FRIENDS!!

WHY DO PEOPLE HAVE TO HATE ME...
...JUST BECAUSE I FELL IN LOVE WITH A MAN?!

WHY DO I HAVE TO GET PUNCHED AND KICKED?!
THEY SPIT AT ME...
...AND LOOK AT ME LIKE I'M SOME-THING DIRTY.

YOU HAVEN'T EXPERIENCED WHAT I'VE BEEN THROUGH!
YOU DON'T KNOW WHAT IT'S LIKE!!

MITCHAN!
BEHIND YOU!!

POLICE.
DROP THE GUN AND PUT YOUR HANDS UP.

YOU'RE UNDER ARREST FOR THE KIDNAPPING OF MINORS, FIREARM VIOLATIONS, AND ATTEMPTED MURDER.

WH...
WHY?

WHY? WE WERE JUST TRYING TO FIND HAPPINESS...

KLANG...

WHY DID YOU HAVE TO RUIN IT?

WUZZ

WUZZ

KOTA YABE CONFESSED TODAY.
THE MONEY WAS FOUND UNDER THE FLOOR AT HIS PLACE OF WORK.

THAT JERK.
HE TRIED TO KEEP ALL THE MONEY FOR HIMSELF.

KOTA WANTED ME TO GIVE YOU A MESSAGE.

"I GOT TO THINKING...
...WHILE I WAS BEING CHASED BY THE COPS.

"WE SAID...
"IF WE USED THIS MONEY...
...WE'D HAVE TO HIDE OUT FOREVER.

"...WE HAD NOTHING...
"...BUT I REALIZE, NOW THAT IT'S TOO LATE...
"...THAT WE HAD FRIENDS WHO UNDERSTOOD US.

"WHEN WE GET OUT OF PRISON...
...LET'S ALL GET TOGETHER AGAIN...
...

"...AND HAVE A DRINK."

TMP
TMP
TMP
MICHIO...

HE ALSO SAID THE BANK ROBBERY WAS HIS IDEA, AND HE ASKED US TO GO EASY ON YOU.
...

LISTEN, EVERYBODY HAS UNFORTUNATE EXPERIENCES...
...EVEN US. SOCIETY DOESN'T LOOK KINDLY ON OUR KIND.
...
BUT YOU KNOW...

...THIS IS THE ONLY LIFE I'VE GOT!!
WE HAVE CONFI-DENCE IN OUR-SELVES!!
WE'RE FABULOUS MISTER LADIES.

HEE HEE
THANK YOU.

BWAZA !!
MINO-RU!!

I SEE...

KOTA AND THE KID...
...BOTH HAD CLEAR EYES.
MORI-GUCHI...
HUH?
YOUR DAD WAS IMPRESSIVE, WASN'T HE?

OH, YEAH...DAD, WHO'S THE WOMAN IN THE PICTURE?!
HUH?
TWITCH
THE ONE IN YOUR POCKET?
SWIP

YEAH...
...I GUESS HE WAS.

THAT'S A PICTURE OF HIROSHI WHEN HE WAS A YOUNG CROSS-DRESSER.
HO HO HO HO
DOOM
NOOOO!!
YOU FOOL! I TOLD YOU IF YOU EVER SHOWED THIS TO OUR SON I'D DIVORCE YOU, DIDN'T I?!
WHAM
WHAM

HE'D HIDDEN IT AWAY? BUT HE LOOKED SO DIFFERENT.
WHAM
WHAM
WAAAAH
PLUP
THIS GUY DIDN'T DO ANYTHING THIS TIME.
STILL SLEEP-ING.
TAKUYA... MINORU ...

Chapter 47 / The End

BABY & Me
Chapter 48
OG

HOW DO I WRITE ABOUT ANOTHER PERSON?

WHY DOES HE WANT US TO WRITE ABOUT SOMEONE WE DON'T KNOW ALL THAT WELL?
HMM ...
WHAT SHOULD I WRITE?

I DON'T EVEN KNOW WHAT SOMEONE WOULD WRITE ABOUT ME.

THE TITLE IS "MY FRIEND."
TAK
THEME
TAK
THE TEACHERS CAME UP WITH THIS IDEA AT A MEETING OF THE 6TH GRADE TEACHERS.

ON TOP OF THAT, TO MAKE SURE EVERYONE GOT WRITTEN ABOUT, OUR TEACHER SPLIT US INTO PAIRS.
ALL RIGHT, I'LL READ OFF THE PAIRS.
YACK
YACK

HMPH! WE'RE NOT LITTLE KIDS.
WHY ARE THEY MAKING US WRITE A COMPOSITION LIKE THIS?
ENDO AND HIRA-TSUKA...
TOMI-SHIMA AND KOBA-YASHI...

GOTOH AND TAMA-DATE...
YIKES.

HEY... GON?
TAMA-DATE
TAMA-DATE
TAMA-DATE
TAMA-DATE
TAMA-DATE
TAMA-DATE
TAMA-DATE

TEACHER ...
YES?
TAMA-DATE FAINTED.
SWOON

AND MY PARTNER IS...
ENOKI AND FUJII...
...SOME-ONE I NEVER WOULD HAVE PICKED.

FU ...

...JI...
...!?!

FUJII ISN'T AN EASY PERSON TO GET TO KNOW.

WUZZ
WUZZ

WUZZ

WHAT ARE YOU LOOKING AT, FUJII?

HUH?
THERE'S A CROW.
ON THAT TREE THERE.

A CROW.

...
KAW

UM... IS IT AN INTERESTING CROW?
HUH?
NOT REALLY, I JUST NOTICED IT WAS THERE.

I SEE THAT, BUT...
OH.

IT SLIPPED.
SWNP

FWAP
FWAP

FWAP FWAP FWAP FWAP

HA HA HA HA
THAT WAS FUNNY. HE LOOKED SO OUTRAGED.
HEE
HEE

WE WERE WATCHING AT JUST THE RIGHT MOMENT...
...WEREN'T WE?

FUJII?
AT THAT MOMENT...
...FUJII WAS JUST SMILING WITH AMUSEMENT...
BUT...

...TO TAKUYA...

HEH

...HE LOOKED BOLD AND MYSTERIOUS.

Fujii comes from a family of six siblings.

IN THE END...

...I COULD ONLY COME UP WITH ONE LINE.
SO? THAT'S OKAY.

NO ...
IT'S NOT OKAY. NO MATTER HOW HARD I TRY, I CAN'T THINK OF WHAT TO WRITE.
WELL, I'VE GOT PLENTY TO SAY ABOUT TAMADATE.
I COULD FILL THIS WHOLE 20-PAGE TABLET.
But that would be a waste of natural resources.

I'M TAKUYA ENOKI. I'M HERE FOR MINORU.
I'M GOTOH. I'M HERE FOR HIROKO.
WUZZ
WUZZ

Author's Note: Part 4

Because I didn't show Kota's face, I received lots of letters from readers who want to know what he looked like. I think not showing his face made Kota more interesting. But you still want to see him, don't you? 💧💧

Notes on Chapter 47

① Actually, Mitchan was a girl at first, but Yusaku, Kota, and Akira were all struggling with problems and I couldn't think of one for Mitchan. So I decided to make her a boy, which would also give me a reason for having those transvestites in the story.

② The story was too long, so we had to pare it down by more than ten pages.

But I did try to make it fit by drawing each panel smaller, you know? Sob

WHEE!
FWIP
FWIP
HUH?
ICHIKA !!
CAN'T YOU WARN US BEFORE YOU DO THAT?!
SH-SHE GAVE ME A HEART ATTACK!
BA-BUMP
BA-BUMP
YEAH.

OH.

UM, ICHIKA...
YES?

I NEED TO FIND OUT SOME THINGS ...
...ABOUT YOUR BROTHER AKIHIRO.
WHY?
WHY? WELL, I JUST DO.

WELL... UM...
HE REALLY LIKES GAMES.
REALLY? GAMES?
HE CAN PLAY PUYOPUYO ON "DIFFICULT" AND GET ALL THE WAY TO SATAN WITHOUT HITTING "CONTINUE" ONCE.
WHAT ?

← As for types of games, that's unknown.

AND THE OTHER DAY, HE WAS SINGING SOMETHING WHILE HE WAS WASHING THE DISHES. I COULDN'T BELIEVE IT WHEN I REALIZED THAT IT WAS "PLEASE SQUEEZE ME" BY FUMIN.
BLAB
AND, UM...HIS IMPERSONATION OF CUTIE HONEY'S "I'M CHANGING ♡" WAS SO BAD I THOUGHT I'D DIE.
BLAB
THEN HE SUDDENLY JUMPED UP AND YELLED, "QUADRUPLE!" AND WHEN HE LANDED, HE TWISTED HIS ANKLE AND HE SEEMED TO BE IN A LOT OF PAIN.
BLAB
REALLY ?
Hello.
GIVE UP, TAKUYA. SHE'LL ONLY CONFUSE YOU MORE.

HEY...

WHADDAYA THINK FUJII'S GONNA WRITE ABOUT YOU?
HUH?

ABOUT ME?
OH YEAH.
I HAVE NO IDEA.

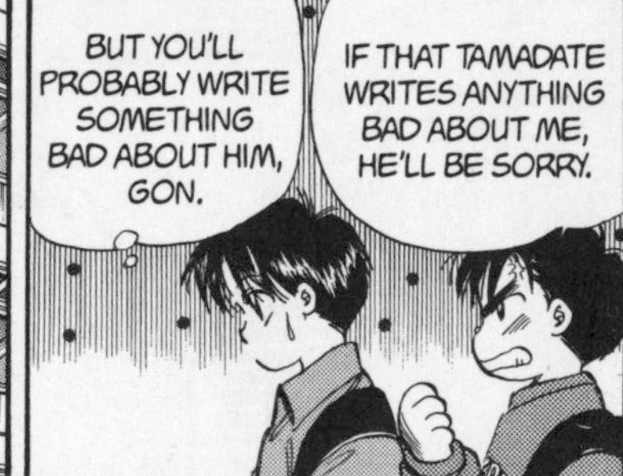
IF THAT TAMADATE WRITES ANYTHING BAD ABOUT ME, HE'LL BE SORRY.
BUT YOU'LL PROBABLY WRITE SOMETHING BAD ABOUT HIM, GON.

THE NEXT DAY
YACK
KONAN ELEMENTARY SCHOOL
YACK

...
WUZZ
WUZZ

SWUMP
I-I COULD ONLY COME UP WITH TWO SEN-TENCES.
I HATE WRITING COMPO-SITIONS !!

AKIHIRO, DID YOU FINISH YOUR PAPER?

PART OF IT.
LET ME SEE.
HMM ...
WHY'S HE READING IT?
FWIP
TAKUYA ...
HUH?
BA BUMP
HEY, THIS IS PRETTY GOOD.
TMP
TMP
TMP
HITOSHI!! HEY!!
KLUNK
LOOK.
FWUP
"TAKUYA ENOKI IS..."
I WANNA READ YOURS, THEN.
TAKE IT EASY.
WHAP
Takuya Enoki is the president of our class.
(omitted)
It is easy to see that he is a good person.

He is always good-natured and easy to talk to.
He always seems to get good scores on his tests, so I think he must have been born smart.

OH NO...

...
THIS MAKES ME SOUND WEIRD.

TAKUYA?

FUJII, YOU HAVE TO REWRITE THIS!
THIS ISN'T ME!!

THEN I GUESS YOU WROTE SOMETHING BETTER ABOUT ME.
GRR

"AKIHIRO FUJII IS ONE OF SIX KIDS. HE ENJOYS PLAYING GAMES."
ONLY TWO SEN-TENCES?
ACK!
WHAM

IS THAT WHAT ICHIKA TOLD YOU YESTER-DAY?

UM, WELL ...
Ichika told him!

I JUST DIDN'T KNOW WHAT TO WRITE ABOUT YOU.

...
OH YEAH? WELL, GUESS WHAT...

YOU'RE ALWAYS SO PERFECT!
THE MORE I WROTE, THE PHONIER IT GOT!

I DON'T UNDERSTAND YOU EITHER.

FINE. I'LL REWRITE IT.
...
SWUP

YOU'RE THINKING TOO HARD.
WHY DON'T YOU JUST RELAX AND WRITE SOMETHING SIMPLE?
SIMPLE?
IT'S NOT LIKE THERE'S A PRIZE INVOLVED. WE'RE NOT EVEN BEING GRADED ON IT.
THAT'S TRUE, BUT...

TAKUY
HUH?

I GET IT!! THAT'S THE DIFFERENCE BETWEEN YOU TWO.
YEAH...
WHAT?
AKIHIRO JUST WANTS TO GET IT DONE...
...AND YOU'RE TRYING FOR PERFECTION.

I'M NOT SAYING THAT AKIHIRO'S WAY IS RIGHT...
...BUT MAYBE YOU SHOULDN'T TAKE IT QUITE SO SERI-OUSLY.

YOU'RE THINKING SO HARD...
...YOU'RE MISSING THE BIG PICTURE.

MORIGUCHI MAKES SENSE, BUT...

...I STILL DON'T LIKE WHAT FUJII WROTE ABOUT ME.

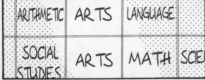

ARITHMETIC	ARTS	LANGUAGE	
SOCIAL STUDIES	ARTS	MATH	SCIE

I PUT A LOT OF EFFORT INTO THIS STUPID COMPOSITION.
I GUESS DIFFERENT PEOPLE DO THINGS DIFFERENTLY.
HEH HEH HEH
THUMP
THUMP

A HAND
RIGHT OR LEFT, IT DOESN'T MATTER.
A HAND

ART...
I'M NOT GOOD AT THIS.
STARE
SPLAT

I...
...I KNEW I WASN'T GOOD AT THIS, SO I CONCENTRATED AND WORKED FAST WITHOUT SAYING A WORD.
THROB
THROB
WOING
A snake...
ha ha ha ha

THEN I SUDDENLY NOTICED...

...THAT THE PEOPLE WHO'D BEEN FOOLING AROUND AT THE BEGINNING HAD DONE AS MUCH OR MORE AS I HAD.
WHY IS THAT?

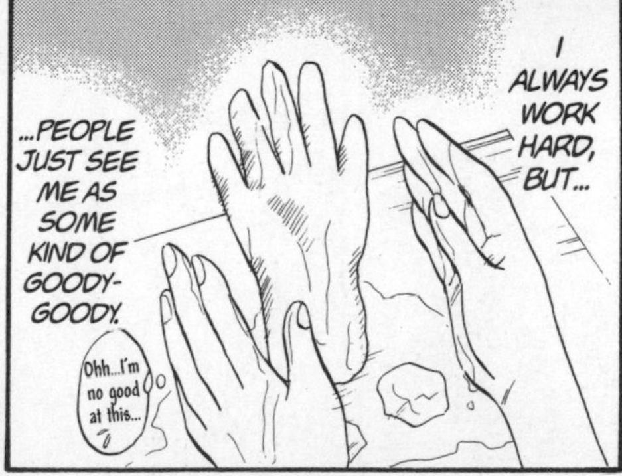
I ALWAYS WORK HARD, BUT...
...PEOPLE JUST SEE ME AS SOME KIND OF GOODY-GOODY.
Ohh...I'm no good at this...

IT LOOKS WEIRD, BUT I DON'T KNOW HOW TO FIX IT.
DON'T GET SO WORKED UP!! LOOK AT MY HAND!!
PAT
PAT

HUH?

FUJII'S SLEEP-ING.
HE'S FINISHED ALREADY? HOW DOES HE DO IT?
WUZZ
WUZZ
Sleeping

...
HOW LUCKY ...

HUH? HOW COME ?
WELL ... FUJII'S SO GOOD AT ART.

ALL RIGHT, LET'S START CLEANING UP.
LINE YOUR HANDS UP IN THE BACK OF THE ROOM.
A HAND
YES, SIR...

WUZZ
WUZZ
TUP

WOW ...
HE'S REALLY GOOD.
They're just elementary school kids, after all.

OH.
MINE'S NO GOOD.
BLINK

YOUR COMPOSITIONS ARE DUE TOMORROW, BUT YOU CAN TURN THEM IN TODAY IF THEY'RE READY.
YIKES

SHOOM

TEACHER, I'M DONE!

WHOA, IT'S SO THICK.
MY MASTER-PIECE IS 20 PAGES LONG.
I ONLY ASKED FOR TWO TO THREE PAGES ...
FWIP

OH, TA-KUYA ...
WIP
GACK

THIS LOOKS LIKE A NOVEL.
YACK
MY MASTERPIECE IS TITLED, "GON: A PRIMITIVE MAN LIVING IN TODAY'S WORLD." I MADE THE COVER WITH MY FAMILY'S PC-98. I ASKED MY FATHER TO WRITE THE POSTSCRIPT.
You wrote all this in one day?
HA HA HA
YACK

WILL YOU COLLECT THE SCHOOL LUNCH QUESTIONNAIRES I PASSED OUT BEFORE THE END OF THE DAY? THOSE WHO FORGOT THEIRS CAN WRITE THEIR SELECTIONS ON A SHEET OF PAPER.
YES, SIR.

TAKUYA MAKES A CLASS LIST IN HIS TABLET AND CHECKS OFF EVERYONE WHO HANDED IN THE FORM.
THAT'S HOW SERIOUS-MINDED HE IS. SCARY.
THROB
THROB

LET'S SEE, NOW...
GUESS I'LL READ THESE.
I'LL START WITH GOTOH'S EPIC.

Tamadate is a boy built on lies. Even his curly bangs are phony.
Whenever he is about to lose in P.E., he fakes a sprained ankle. But he is such a bad actor that all I can do is hold my stomach and laugh.
I hear he wants to be a TV star when he grows up, but his singing is so bad, again, all I can do is hold my stomach and laugh. (The rest is omitted.)

Amazingly, descendants of Java Man still exist, and one of them lives right here in Kumanoi City. His name is Tadashi Gotoh, nicknamed "Gon." His intelligence is close to that of modern man, but the primitive genes are still quite evident in his appearance. The gorilla-like face, the short legs... (The rest is omitted.)

HMM ...
WELL ...
...THIS ISN'T FOR A GRADE, BUT...

TEACHERS TODAY...
...ARE CONCERNED ABOUT CHILDREN'S ABILITY TO UNDERSTAND AND ACCEPT OTHERS.

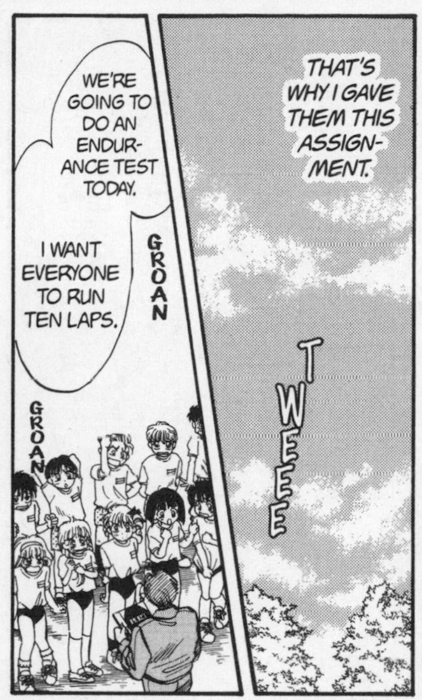
THAT'S WHY I GAVE THEM THIS ASSIGNMENT.
TWEEE
WE'RE GOING TO DO AN ENDURANCE TEST TODAY.
I WANT EVERYONE TO RUN TEN LAPS.
GROAN
GROAN

TMP
TMP
TMP

TEN LAPS? I'M GONNA DIE...
I'M GETTING A STITCH IN MY SIDE...
WEEZ
WEEZ
HUFF
HUFF

WHAT? ARE YOU ALL RIGHT?
YEAH... JUST THREE MORE LAPS...
I THOUGHT YOU WERE GOOD AT RUNNING.
NOT LONG DISTANCE ...
HUFF
HUFF

HEY... TAKUYA ...
HOW MANY TIMES HAVE WE MET LIKE THIS?
HOW MANY MORE LAPS, GON?
ANOTHER FIVE AND A HALF FOR ME.
WEEZ
WEEZ
HUFF
HUFF
HUFF
BUT TAMADATE STILL HAS SEVEN LAPS TO GO.
WHAT? HE'S ONLY RUN THREE LAPS?
...
HUFF
HUFF
HUFF
HUFF
TROMP
TROMP
!!
HUFF
AKIHIRO!! WHAT'RE YOU WALKING FOR?
OUCH ...
I MIGHT AS WELL. I'M ALMOST DONE.
WHAP
HUFF
HUFF
HUH ?
HOW MANY MORE LAPS DO YOU HAVE?
LAPS?
TWO, I GUESS.
WEEZ
HUFF
I'M A GONER...
SWIP

HUH?
HUFF
WHY ARE YOU HOLDING YOUR SIDE? DOES IT HURT?
WEEZ

YEAH ...
HUFF
BUT I THINK IT'LL GO AWAY IF I KEEP RUNNING...

DON'T KILL YOURSELF. JUST WALK.
FINISHING FAST DOESN'T MEAN ANYTHING. YOU JUST HAVE TO WAIT FOR EVERYBODY ELSE.
HUFF
WEEZ

...
HUFF

I'M...
I'M NOT LIKE YOU, FUJII.

TMP TMP TMP
HUFF

WHAT'S WITH HIM?
TAKUYA'S BEEN SNAPPING AT YOU ALL DAY.
DID YOU DO SOME-THING TO HIM?
WEEZ
WEEZ
I DON'T KNOW ...

TWO MORE LAPS...
AND HE DOESN'T EVEN LOOK TIRED.

BUT HE WASN'T IN ANY HURRY TO FINISH.
WHY?

WHY IS EVERYTHING SO EASY FOR HIM?
I FEEL LIKE A FOOL FOR TRYING SO HARD...
OH...
I'M POOPED.
WEEN
WEEN

IT'S JUST NOT MY DAY.

...
GASP
SHWOOSH

OH, YOU'RE AWAKE.
UM... WHERE... AM I?
YOU'RE IN THE NURSE'S OFFICE.

WHAT TIME IS IT?!
IT'S ALL RIGHT. FIFTH PERIOD JUST ENDED.

BUT...THE END-OF-THE-DAY MEETING'S ABOUT TO START!
WHAT'LL I DO?!

I DIDN'T COLLECT THE QUESTION-NAIRES!!

I COL-LECTED THEM FOR YOU.

HUFF
HUFF

WUZZ
WUZZ

WHAT?

YOU HEARD ME.
I COL-LECTED THEM.

WHY?
THE TEACHER ASKED ME TO.
HUFF
I was standing right in front of him.

DID EVERYBODY HAND THEM IN?
I DON'T KNOW. BUT THERE ARE ELEVEN HERE.
HUFF
HUFF
ELEVEN...

THAT'S ALL OF THEM.
UM...
THANKS.

?
WHEN-EVER I...

NO MATTER HOW MANY TIMES I REMIND THEM...
...SOME-BODY ALWAYS FOR-GETS.

Wip

...
HEY!
TMP TMP TMP

HOLD ON A MINUTE ...
...ENOKI.
TMP TMP TMP
YACK
YACK

WHAT'S YOUR PROBLEM?! YOU'VE BEEN IN A BAD MOOD ALL DAY! WHAT DID I DO TO YOU?!
YOU DIDN'T DO ANYTHING!!
TMP TMP TMP TMP

UH...
Wip

HOW COME YOU DON'T DO ANYTHING...
...BUT YOU CAN DO EVERY-THING?!
YOU SHOULD BE THE CLASS PRESI-DENT.
I CAN'T DO ANY-THING!
WHEN I LOOK AT YOU...
...SOMETIMES I GET SO FRUSTRATED!!
I'M NOT SUCH A GOOD BOY.
UH-OH...
I GET GOOD SCORES ON MY TESTS BECAUSE I STUDY HARD THE NIGHT BEFORE.
YOU AND I ARE SO DIFFER-ENT.

I HAVE TO WORK EXTRA HARD JUST TO KEEP UP.
THAT STUFF YOU WROTE DIDN'T SOUND LIKE ME AT ALL.
IT MADE ME SOUND WEIRD...LIKE I WASN'T HUMAN OR SOMETHING.
ANYWAY...
I ENVY YOU.
EN...
ENVY...
...ME?
WHY?!
I ENVY YOU MORE!!
HUH?
YOU REALLY THINK...
...THINGS ARE EASY FOR ME?
WELL
...

YOU'RE WRONG.
SWUMP!
HUFF
FUJII?
IF I WAS THAT GOOD AT THINGS, I'D TRY A LOT HARDER.
IT MAY LOOK LIKE I'M NOT TRYING HARD, BUT THAT'S JUST THE WAY I AM!!

VEEN

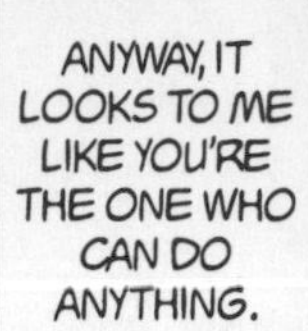
ANYWAY, IT LOOKS TO ME LIKE YOU'RE THE ONE WHO CAN DO ANYTHING.

GULP
ME?
BUT I THOUGHT THERE WAS SOMETHING WRONG WHEN I WAS WRITING THAT COMPOSITION.

IT'S KINDA FUNNY, HUH?
HEH

?
WE MAKE JUDGMENTS ABOUT PEOPLE ALL THE TIME, BUT WHEN WE FIND OUT HOW OTHERS SEE US, WE GET UPSET.

OH.
AT THAT MOMENT ...
...I SUDDENLY UNDERSTOOD WHY THE TEACHER HAD GIVEN US THIS ASSIGNMENT AND WHY IT WASN'T FOR A GRADE.

BUT I STILL ENVY FUJII.

I GUESS YOU'RE HUMAN AFTER ALL, FUJII.

WHAT'S THAT SUP-POSED TO MEAN?

STAFF ROOM

WELL ...
THESE STUDENTS ...
...CER-TAINLY HAVE DISTINCT PERSON-ALITIES.

Takuya Enoki works hard at everything.
MINORU, WHAT DO YOU WANT TO EAT TONIGHT?

UM...POT SNICKOS.
POT STICK-ERS?
I think he works hardest at taking care of his little brother.

But to an outsider, they just look like a couple of carefree kids.
THEN LET'S GO TO THE SUPER-MARKET AND BUY SOME.
POT SNICKOS! ♡

I was jealous of Akihiro Fujii because I thought he could do anything.
I thought he was cool and wise, but I found out he's not so different from everybody else.
DARN. DARN.
WHY AREN'T THEY GOING IN?
STOP THAT.
IT'S A WASTE OF OUR NATURAL RE-SOURCES.
6-2

MAYBE CHILDREN ARE BETTER...
...AT READING PEOPLE THAN ADULTS ARE.

Chapter 48 / The End

BABY & Me
Chapter 49

EDOMAE!!
WUZZ
WUZZ

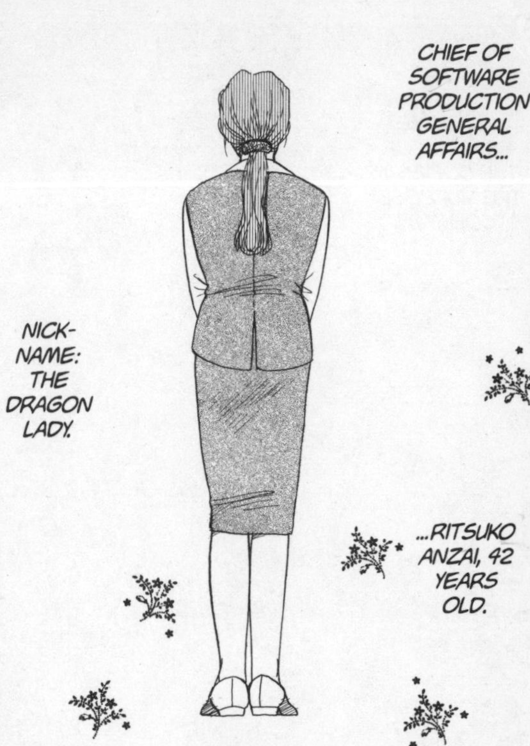
CHIEF OF SOFTWARE PRODUCTION GENERAL AFFAIRS...
NICK-NAME: THE DRAGON LADY.
...RITSUKO ANZAI, 42 YEARS OLD.

GULP...

WH-WHAT IS IT, MS. ANZAI?
YOU'VE BEEN MAKING A LOT OF PHOTOCOPIES LATELY.
LET'S START WITH THESE 150 COPIES.
WHAT WERE THEY FOR?

I WAS PREPARING SOME BLUEPRINTS FOR A CLIENT.
MUNCH MUNCH
I SEE.
AND WHAT ABOUT THESE EIGHT?

THIS IS... UM...
UH-OH. I WAS MAKING COPIES OF ANIME SONG LYRICS.
MUNCH MUNCH
...

STOP EATING WHEN I'M TALKING TO YOU!!
YES, MA'AM!!

THOSE WERE...UM... SORRY. I DON'T REMEMBER.
HMPH!
YOU'RE SUPPOSED TO NOTE THE REASON FOR THE COPIES IN THE "PURPOSE" COLUMN!!
KLAK
UH...YES.

SOUNDS LIKE ANOTHER PEACEFUL DAY AT THE OFFICE.
PHEW
OH, MR. ENOKI, WELCOME BACK.

I HOPE YOU'LL HAVE A WORD WITH YOUR PEOPLE AS WELL.
HUH?

THE TEAM ON THIS FLOOR IS UNUSUALLY WASTEFUL.
REALLY?

WELL, EDOMAE AND THE OTHERS ON THE A TEAM ARE WORKING ON AN IMPORTANT PROJECT, SO THEY NEED A LOT OF OFFICE SUPPLIES.
I REALIZE THAT. BUT THE A TEAM HAD BETTER KEEP AN EYE ON THE OTHER TEAM.
Give us a break?

OTHER TEAM?
UH...MS. ANZAI...
WHAT IS IT?
KLAK
KLAK

I NEED TWO FOLDERS, A BOX EACH OF RED AND BLACK PENS, AND SOME GLUE.
...
YOU NEED THEM TODAY?
IF POS-SIBLE.

ALL RIGHT. I'LL DROP THEM OFF LATER.
SHE MAKES YOU NERVOUS JUST TO ASK FOR THE SUPPLIES YOU NEED.
PHEW

I SWEAR MS. ANZAI'S GOT IT IN FOR ME.
Sheesh.
GRUMBLE
GRUMBLE
IT'S 'CAUSE YOU LOOK LIKE A GOOF-OFF.

BUT THOSE GIRLS ON THE B TEAM ARE EVEN WORSE THAN WE ARE.
YEAH.
YACK
YACK

HUH?
WHAT'S THIS?!
SWUP
HEY!
TMP TMP
CHIEF!
WHAT?

SHE'S GOT A FILE FULL OF PICTURES OF SMAP*.
Nooo!! Please, Ms. Ōmori ...
THIS ONE HAS CUTOUTS OF SOCCER PLAYERS.
I need that!
THIS ONE'S DESK IS FULL OF TOILET PAPER!
Hi

*A Japanese boy band.

WE'RE GETTING BLAMED FOR YOU GUYS' WASTEFULNESS!!
WAAH
HOW COULD YOU?! BULLIES !!
YOU DON'T HAVE TO BE LIKE MS. ANZAI TO WANT TO SCOLD THEM.
Those belong to the company.
MS. ANZAI IS A HARD WORKER.

!!
WUZZ
WUZZ

WUZZ
WUZZ
MS. ANZAI ...

MAY I SIT HERE?
CERTAINLY, IF YOU DON'T MIND.

MIND ?
OF COURSE I DON'T MIND.

OH...
WELL, NONE OF THE OTHERS LIKE TO SIT WITH ME.
SMILE

...
OH, A HOMEMADE LUNCH. HOW NICE.
HA HA...
WELL, I AM A WIFE, AFTER ALL. IT'S IMPORTANT TO ECONOMIZE WHERE YOU CAN.
I MAKE MY OWN LUNCH WHEN I MAKE THE OTHERS.

Author's Note: Part 5

Let's see... Oh yeah. Readers often ask me if there is any character merchandise available for Baby and Me, and I can tell you absolutely, positively that there is unequivocally **none.** And if there were, it probably wouldn't sell. óò

BUT ...
A NORMAL LUNCH ISN'T GOOD ENOUGH FOR KIDS THESE DAYS.
IF THE FOOD'S NOT EXCITING ENOUGH, THEY COMPLAIN.

REALLY? IN MY DAY, WE ATE RICE AND NORI*.
OH, YOU HAVE A SCRAMBLED-EGG ROLL TOO.
WOULD YOU LIKE SOME?
HUH ?!
A-ARE YOU SURE?
PLEASE HAVE SOME.
I'm not forcing it on you.

*sheets of seaweed, like on sushi.

I MADE HER FEEL LIKE SHE HAD TO OFFER IT TO ME.
THANK YOU.
MUNCH

THROB
THROB
OH ...
THIS IS REALLY ...

I DON'T KNOW IF IT'S ANY GOOD.
I'M NOT A VERY GOOD COOK.
... DELICIOUS!!

HUH?!
HUH? DID YOU SAY SOMETHING?
NO.
IT'S SO FLAVORFUL. YOU PUT SOUP STOCK IN IT.
YOUR FAMILY MUST LOVE YOUR COOKING.
OH, NO ...
THEY'VE NEVER SAID SO, ANYWAY.

REALLY? MAYBE THEY'RE JUST TOO SHY TO TELL YOU.
I REALLY DON'T KNOW.
CHIEF ENOKI, DO YOU BELIEVE THAT A WOMAN'S PLACE IS IN THE HOME?

HUH? IT DOESN'T ...
... REALLY MATTER TO ME.

DOESN'T MATTER ?
WELL, I'M A TYPE B PERSON, SO I'M PRETTY EASY.

I'D LET THE WOMAN DECIDE.
SHE COULD STAY HOME OR HAVE A CAREER, AS LONG AS SHE WAS HAPPY.
KLAK
KLAK

MY WIFE STAYED HOME, BUT...
...SHE SEEMED TO LIKE IT.

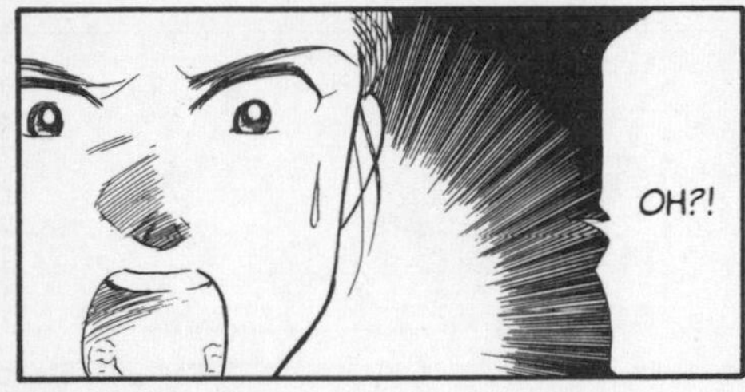
OH?!

SO WHAT YOU REALLY MEAN IS...
...A WOMAN WOULD BE HAPPIER STAYING HOME, ISN'T THAT RIGHT?!
KLUNK
GASP
WHUP

THAT'S NOT WHAT I MEANT.
YES IT IS!! OF COURSE IT'S HARD FOR A WOMAN TO BALANCE WORK AND HOUSE-WORK...
MUMBLE

HELP OUT?
BUT HOUSE-WORK IS THE WOMAN'S JOB!

BUT STAYING HOME IS STIFLING!
HARD? IT'S PROBABLY IMPOSSIBLE UNLESS HER FAMILY HELPS OUT.
WUMP...

...
WHAT...
...ARE YOU TALK-ING ABOUT ?

HAVE I...
...MADE A MISTAKE?

SHAKE
SHAKE
Mr. Enoki
Ms. Anzai
I GUESS THE CHIEF'S A MAN, AFTER ALL.
SHAKE
UGH...
SHAKE
PHEW
CHIEF ENOKI AND MS. ANZAI SEEM TO BE HAVING A NICE CHAT.

BECAUSE MS. ANZAI'S SO SERIOUS, SHE'S BECOME THE OFFICE ENFORCER, BUT...
... MAYBE ...

...SHE'S NOT...
...AS TOUGH AS SHE SEEMS.

DAD...
THE BATH-ROOM'S FREE.

I WAS PLAYING WITH MINORU, SO THE WATER'S A LITTLE LOW.
OKAY.

THEN ...
GUESS I'LL TAKE A BATH.
RUSTLE
RUSTLE

OH...
TAKUYA ...
HUH?
SWUFF
SWUFF

DO YOU THINK ...
...A MOTHER SHOULD STAY HOME?

HUH?

DOES IT BOTHER YOU THAT THERE'S NO MOTHER HERE WHEN YOU GET HOME FROM SCHOOL?
HUH? WHAT?

I...
WHY SHOULD IT BOTHER ME?! I CAN TAKE CARE OF MYSELF!!

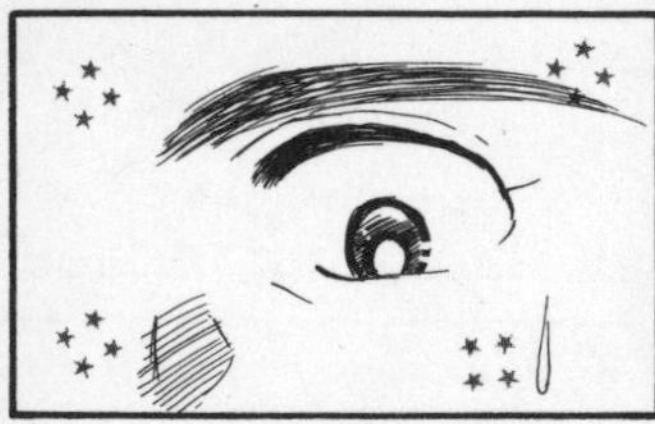

YEAH, YOU CAN--
RIGHT!

HE'S RIGHT. FAMILIES ARE DIFFERENT TODAY.

WHY DID DAD SAY THAT?
IS HE TRYING TO TELL ME...

...HE'S FOUND A NEW MOTHER FOR US?!

KSHHHH
THERE'S NOT ENOUGH WATER.

WUZZ
WUZZ

THE INSTANT COFFEE COUNT ISN'T MATCHING UP LATELY.
Single-serving packet
COFFEE

YOU'RE NOT SUPPOSED TO TAKE THEM HOME.

KLAK KLAK

UH-OH, I'VE BEEN TAKING ONE HOME EVERY DAY.

UH-OH. THE DRAGON LADY'S BEEN COUNTING THEM.

SHE'S REALLY TAKES HER JOB SERIOUSLY.

WHISPER WHISPER

WUZZ WUZZ

ENOKI...

YES, MR. YAMAZAKI?

I'LL BE MEETING WITH MR. YAMABE FROM MEC THIS EVENING. HE WANTS TO SEE HOW FAR ALONG WE ARE.

OKAY. BUT THE BLUEPRINTS ARE AT MY HOUSE.
HE'LL BE HERE A LITTLE AFTER 6:00. CAN YOU HAVE THEM HERE BY THEN?
I COULD HAVE MY SON BRING THEM. HE GETS HOME AROUND 3:00, SO THEY SHOULD BE HERE IN TIME.
PLEASE TRY.

WAAH
IT'S NOT FAIR!!

WAAH
HIC
HIC
WHAT'S WRONG?
YOU SCARED ME.

LISTEN, EDOMAE!!
WIP
DOOM
THAT WITCH! I CAN'T STAND HER!!

I GAVE HER MY RECEIPTS, BUT SHE SAID SHE WOULDN'T ALLOW ANY THAT WEREN'T SPECIFICALLY LABELED!
...

HOW COULD SHE?! I CAN'T REMEMBER SOME OF THEM!
I NEED THAT MONEY!
WAAAH
THAT OLD HAG!!

HIRAMATSU, COME HERE.
WIP
WIP
SNIFF
YES?

FIRST OF ALL, YOU SHOULDN'T TALK ABOUT PEOPLE LIKE THAT.
WITH THE ECONOMY LIKE IT IS, THE PRESIDENT EXPECTS MS. ANZAI TO ACCOUNT FOR EVERY YEN.
BUT WHAT ABOUT THE STUFF I CAN'T REMEMBER?
THAT'S YOUR RESPONSIBILITY. JUST WRITE SOMETHING THAT SEEMS RIGHT ON THE RECEIPTS.
IF SHE HAD HUNDREDS OF UNIDENTIFIED RECEIPTS TO ACCOUNT FOR, MS. ANZAI WOULD BE IN BIG TROUBLE.
OH...
?
WHAT'S GOING ON?

RRING
CHIEF ENOKI, YOUR SONS ARE DOWN IN THE LOBBY.
OKAY. TELL THEM I'LL BE RIGHT THERE.
SIR, THEY'RE HERE.
OH, THANK GOODNESS.

WUZZ
TAKUYA ...
MINO-RU...
WUZZ
HEY, DAD.
HI!
HELLO, BOYS.
SO YOU'RE MR. ENOKI'S SONS.
RUFF
THANK YOU VERY MUCH.
YOU'RE GOOD BOYS.
RUFF
AND YOU'RE HANDSOME TOO. I BOUGHT SOME CANDY JUST FOR YOU.
DAD...
IT'S OKAY. HE'S HARM-LESS.
I CAN'T BELIEVE CHIEF ENOKI HAS A SON THAT BIG.
THEY'RE SO CUTE. ♡
DOOM

OMORI...
THE CHIEF AND MS. ANZAI HAVE GOTTEN PRETTY CHUMMY.
GRR
GRR
GRR
THAT'S A LIE!!
THE CHIEF'S NOT LIKE THAT!!
WILL YOU HAVE DINNER WITH ME?
WOOSH
SORRY. THERE'S A SHOW I HAVE TO WATCH.
WHAT?!
DING
COME ON, OMORI ...
WOOSH
JUST SHUT UP, OKAY?!
HUH?
OH !!
TAKUYA AND MINORU. ♡

HOW HAVE YOU BEEN? WHAT ARE YOU DOING HERE?
HEY.
WE HAD TO DROP SOMETHING OFF FOR OUR DAD.
UBB...
I'LL HAVE DINNER WITH YOU, EDOMAE, BUT IT'S YOUR TREAT.
YIPPEE!

TAKUYA, THERE'S SOME-THING I WANT TO ASK YOU.
WILL YOU HAVE DINNER WITH US?
WHAT ...?
PAT

Five Star Restaurant
Open Every Day
HAS YOUR FATHER BEEN ACTING... STRANGE LATELY?

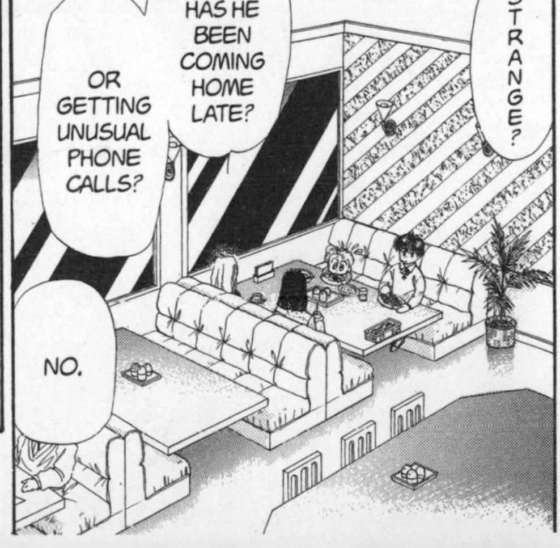
STRANGE?
HAS HE BEEN COMING HOME LATE?
OR GETTING UNUSUAL PHONE CALLS?
NO.

BUT ...
HE DID ASK ME IF I'D LIKE TO HAVE A STAY-AT-HOME MOM.
WHAT ?!

THAT'S A RED FLAG.
WHY?
SLURP

PHEW...

I CAN FINALLY GO HOME...

1 2 3 4 5 6
DING

MS. ANZAI?

?
YES?

WHAT DO YOU MEAN?
HA HA... WOMEN ARE SO PRO-TEAN.

SIGH

TIRED?
WHAT?

WELL, I...
I HAVE A LOT ON MY PLATE, I SUPPOSE.

...

LET'S HAVE A DRINK!
HUH?
JUST FOR HALF AN HOUR.
WHAK

BAR Castle
IT'S NO FUN...
...BEING A WOMAN.

NO?
AT WORK...

...AS A WIFE ...
...AS A MOTHER ...
...I NEVER FEEL...
...LIKE I'M APPRECI-ATED.

FOR A MOMENT, I FELT A PANG.
SUDDENLY I COULD HEAR..

...MY OWN MOTHER SAYING THOSE SAME WORDS.

OH, I'M SORRY.
HUH?

I DON'T MEAN TO COMPLAIN SO MUCH.
THAT'S NO FUN, IS IT?
IT'S OKAY.

YOU'RE NOT WHAT I EXPECTED. NOTHING RATTLES YOU.

I GUESS IT'S 'CAUSE YOU'RE OLD.

SHUNK

I'LL TAKE THAT AS A COMPLIMENT.

I SUPPOSE MOST PEOPLE THESE DAYS WOULD HEAD FOR A KARAOKE BAR NOW.

NOT ME.

NO?

I'M AN OLD MAN, REMEMBER?

GOODBYE, TAKUYA AND MINORU.
WUZZ
WUZZ
BYE. THANKS FOR DINNER.

WUZZ
MINORU? WHAT'S WRONG?
WUZZ
WAAH!! I SEEPY...

!!

HEY! THERE'S THE CHIEF.
OH!

▲ Minoru's down here.

EDOMAE ...
YES?

DON'T BE LATE FOR WORK TOMORROW.
HUH?

GOOD NIGHT, CHIEF ENOKI.
UH, GOOD NIGHT, MS. ANZAI.

KLAK
KLAK
BUSINESS HOTEL

SHE'S WALKING AWAY LIKE NOTHING HAPPENED...
NOTHING DID HAPPEN.

KLAKA
KLAKA

DAD, YOU'RE A JERK!!
ZZZ
ZZZ

YEAH...

NOTHING HAPPENED...

...BUT RUMORS ARE SURE TO SPREAD THROUGH THE OFFICE LIKE WILDFIRE.

TAKUYA, I'M TELLING YOU, IT'S NOT TRUE.

HEY

I'M ASLEEP!!

BWAZA...

CHEEP

KLAK
KLAK

GOOD MORNING...

GOOD MORNING. SERVE THE SOUP, PLEASE.

NO.

I DON'T WANT ANYTHING TO EAT.

SNAP

WOOSH*

*Sound of refrigerator door opening.

AGAIN?!
IS THAT MY LUNCH?

YOU DON'T HAVE TO MAKE LUNCH FOR ME ANYMORE. I'LL BUY MY LUNCH. CAN I HAVE SOME MONEY?
DO YOU KNOW HOW MUCH MONEY THAT IS IN A MONTH?!
BLUP BLUP BLUP

IT'S EMBARRASSING TO TAKE A LUNCH TO SCHOOL.

WHAT?
IT'S JUST LUNCH MONEY. YOU BOTH WORK. ARE WE THAT POOR?

I DON'T WORK BECAUSE WE'RE POOR!!
WHAM
O-OKAY, TAKE IT EASY.

WHAT'S ALL THE SCREAMING ABOUT?
THIS CHILD DOESN'T WANT TO TAKE HER LUNCH TO SCHOOL ANYMORE.

WHAT? IS THAT ALL?
IS THAT ALL?

NEVER MIND THAT, RITSUKO ...

YOU GOT HOME LATE LAST NIGHT.

I HAD TO WORK LATE.
ANYWAY, IT WASN'T VERY LATE. I WAS HOME BY 10:00.
YES, BUT I HAD TO MAKE MY OWN DINNER. YOU KNOW I DON'T LIKE THAT.
BUT... YOU COME HOME WHENEVER YOU WANT.
AND RYOKO'S A GIRL. SHE CAN MAKE DINNER.
WHAT? ME? NO WAY.
COOKING IS A WIFE'S JOB.

THAT WAS ONE OF THE CONDITIONS FOR YOU GETTING A JOB.

IF YOU CAN'T HANDLE IT, YOU'D BETTER QUIT.

WH-WHAT ...?

WHAT AM I TO YOU TWO?!

IT'S NO FUN ...
...BEING A WOMAN.
AS A WIFE...
...AS A MOTHER...
...I NEVER FEEL LIKE I'M APPRECI-ATED.

I'M SORRY. PLEASE FORGIVE ME.
NO.
DITH ITH YUMMY.
BOW
BOW

Chapter 49 / The End

BABY & ME
Chapter 50

YO.

WUZZ
WHAT?
WUZZ

NO WAY...
BUT ISN'T MS. ANZAI MARRIED?

I HEARD SHE'S BEEN COMING ON TO HIM...
YIKES...

WIP
HIDE
HIDE

...

GEEZ...
THE RUMORS ARE ALREADY FLYING.

CHIEF ENOKI ...
MS. ANZAI ...
I'M GLAD I CAUGHT YOU.
DO YOU HAVE A MINUTE?
RATTLE
SWSHH
HERE.
THIS IS FOR YOU.
MS. ANZAI, WHAT'S ...?
IT'S JUST A BOX LUNCH.
THERE'S NO HIDDEN MEANING TO IT.

I'D BE IN TROUBLE IF THERE WERE.
WELL, THANK YOU.
I MADE IT THIS MORNING, BUT NOBODY WANTED IT.
MY DAUGHTER...
...WOULDN'T TAKE IT.

YOUR HAIR...
HUH?
YOU SHOULD WEAR IT LOOSE.
IT LOOKED GOOD LAST NIGHT.

IT GETS IN THE WAY...
...WHEN I'M WORKING.
I SEE.
THAT'S ...
...JUST LIKE YOU.
WELL, GOOD-BYE.

WELL?! HOW DO I LOOK?!
WHAT ABOUT ME?!
DO I LOOK GOOD WITH MY HAIR LOOSE?!
WHAT ?!
CHIEF !!
DOOM

THERE SEEM TO BE SOME BASELESS RUMORS ABOUT MS. ANZAI AND ME FLOATING AROUND.
UM, MAYBE.
SO I'D APPRECIATE IT IF YOU TWO DIDN'T TELL ANYONE ABOUT LAST NIGHT.
LAST NIGHT? YOU MEAN...
GULP
YOU TWO HAVE IT ALL WRONG.
MS. ANZAI AND I JUST HAD ONE DRINK TOGETHER!!
IF THAT'S ALL IT WAS, WHY ARE YOU WORRIED? GUILTY CONSCIENCE?
I SAID, NOTHING HAPPENED! HOW MANY TIMES DO I HAVE TO TELL YOU THAT?!
BUT IT'S NO USE JUST TALKING TO US.
YEAH.
WHY NOT?
'CAUSE THE WALKING LOUD-SPEAKER IS HERE.
THEY'RE HAVING AN AFFAIR?
YACK
YACK
DEFI-NITELY!
THE CHIEF'S JUST TRYING TO PROTECT HER.

ELEMENTARY SCHOOL
HMM ...

I CAN UNDERSTAND HOW YOU FEEL, TAKUYA...
...BUT YOUR DAD IS A MAN, AND HE'S NOT THAT OLD.

IT'D BE SAD IF HE WAS ALWAYS ALONE.
HE SHOULD GET REMARRIED SOMEDAY.

OF COURSE ...
I DON'T WANT HIM TO BE ALONE FOREVER.
THEN WHY DON'T YOU JUST TELL HIM, "CONGRATU-LATIONS!"?
HO HO HO

'CAUSE I CAN'T STAND THE THOUGHT OF IT!!
THWAK
GACK
WHOA!

SOMEDAY I'LL BE OKAY WITH IT...
...BUT NOT NOW!

WHY NOT?
...

WELL...
SWFF

Author's Note: Part 6

Chapters 49 and 50 are dedicated to the mothers of the world. Of course, I hope that children will read them too.

I include myself in this, but kids sometimes say terribly hurtful things to their parents. Now that I'm grown, I regret a lot of the cruel things I said as a child. Tsk, tsk... But I was just a kid...

Notes on Chapter 50

My assistants told me that Takuya's dad looked sort of like a pervert when he got on the elevator with Ms. Anzai. Hmm... That's perverted?

How weird...

I'M GONNA GO FIND OUT!!
TAKUYA, COME BACK!!
ZAK ZAK ZAK

DID YOU HEAR?
W·C

KLAK

I WONDER HOW LONG SHE INTENDS TO KEEP WORKING?
PROBABLY TO RETIREMENT AGE.
I WOULDN'T WANT TO WORK WITH A LOT OF YOUNG GIRLS IF I WERE HER AGE, THOUGH.

THROWING MYSELF AT HIM?

WOOSH
KSHHHH

WE'D BETTER GET BACK TO WORK.
YEAH, GOOD IDEA.

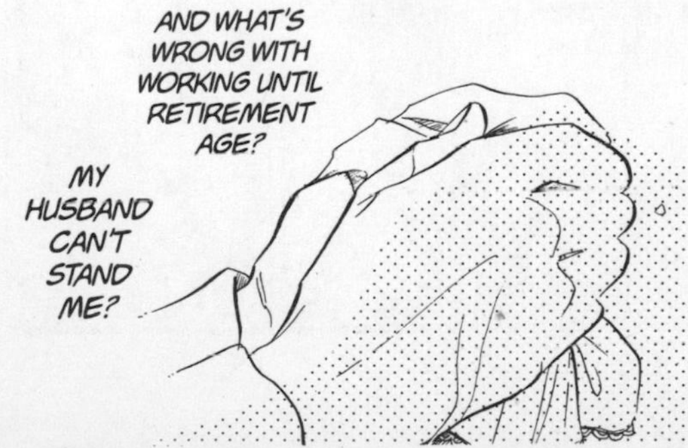
THOSE STUPID GIRLS...
IS THAT WHAT THEY THINK?
AND WHAT'S WRONG WITH WORKING UNTIL RETIREMENT AGE?
MY HUSBAND CAN'T STAND ME?

OH...
HEH...
I HAVE GOTTEN OLD.
I DON'T UNDERSTAND.
THE HARDER I WORK...
...THE MORE THEY HATE ME.
KLAK
OH.
A bean jam bun for dessert.
THIS LOOKS DELICIOUS. ♡
THANKS FOR THE LUNCH.
MY HUSBAND ...
...AND EVEN MY DAUGHTER ...
ISN'T THERE...
...ANYONE WHO...?
WUZZ
WUZZ

Author's Note: Part 7

My "Marimo Ragawa's Let Me Draw What I Want" section in volume 8 got good reviews. I didn't have room for it in this volume, but I'll save a page in the next one.

▨ Regarding my fan letters: Thank you very much for all your letters, but a word of caution. Please don't send things like cards or comics for me to autograph or to draw illustrations on. (Or money.) I can't be responsible for them. I'm sorry.

This may sound mean, but I get letters from a lot of people and I really can't give anyone special treatment. Please try to understand. BOW

Well, that's it for volume 9. See you again in volume 10! (Oh, I'm into double digits. Hooray!)

OH, YOU...
AREN'T YOU...
...CHIEF ENOKI'S BOYS?
WHAT ARE YOU DOING HERE?
WAITING FOR YOUR FATHER?
KLAK
NO, UH...
UM ...
YES.
OH, MY...
HUH?
HOW ADORABLE!
WHUP
HUH?
I WONDER IF SHE LIKES KIDS...
STARE
HOW OLD ARE YOU?
GASP
ME'S TWO.
IS THAT SO?

DON'T ...
...TRY TO WIN MINORU OVER!!
SWUP
WIN HIM OVER ?
WHAT...
WHAT DO YOU WANT WITH OUR FATHER?!

HUH?
I DON'T ...

TRIP
FWUMP

I DON'T WANT HIM TO GET REMAR-RIED!!

SHOOM

OUCH...
ZING ZING
ARE YOU ALL RIGHT?
KLAK KLAK KLAK
BWAZA !!

OH...
YOU'RE BLEEDING.

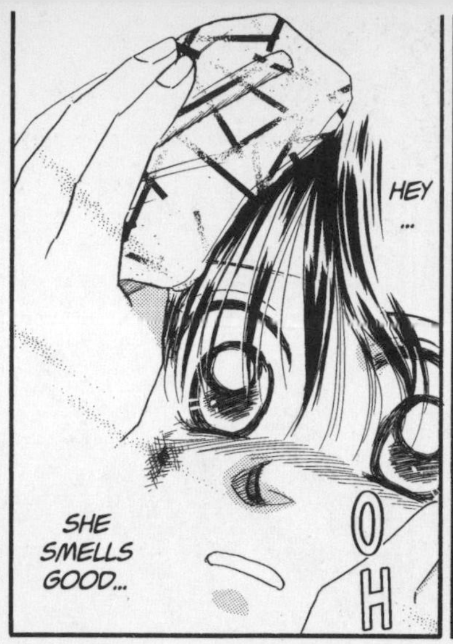
HEY ...
OH
SHE SMELLS GOOD...

YOU DON'T HAVE TO WORRY.
?

I HAVE ...
...A HUSBAND AND A DAUGH-TER.

YOU DO?
BE-SIDES ...
...I'M TOO OLD FOR YOUR FATHER.

I'D FEEL SORRY FOR HIM IF HE WERE IN LOVE...
...WITH AN OLD WOMAN LIKE ME.
EVERY-ONE WOULD MAKE FUN OF HIM.

...
I'M SORRY.

?
FOR WHAT?

WELL...
I MADE A MISTAKE, BUT YOU'RE THE ONE SAYING BAD THINGS ABOUT YOURSELF.
YOU...

...SEEM UNHAPPY.

BUBBLE FIVE
I CAME HOME EARLY FOR THEM.
WHERE ARE THOSE KIDS?

THANK YOU.
HUH?

A REALLY GOOD CHILD...
...ISN'T ONE WHO GETS GOOD GRADES AND NEVER CAUSES TROUBLE.
IT'S ONE WHO UNDERSTANDS THE PAIN OF OTHERS.

CHIEF ENOKI IS A LUCKY MAN.
WUZN
WUZN

...

BWAZA?

WHAK
HUH?

I'M HOME.
I HOME!
WHERE HAVE YOU TWO BEEN?
TAKUYA, WHAT HAP-PENED TO YOU?!
I FELL DOWN.

SLOSH
SLOSH
SHARP 3.6

RYOKO ...
PLEASE GET OUT OF THE WAY.
WHUP

YOU'RE GONNA DO THE LAUNDRY NOW?
THUD
WHAT OTHER TIME IS THERE?

HEY...
OH.
WEL-COME HOME.

YOU'RE HANGING THOSE OUT NOW?

DON'T. IT'S EMBAR-RASSING.

IF YOU HANG THAT STUFF OUT AT NIGHT...
...PEOPLE WILL THINK YOU'RE CRAZY.

HOW LONG ...
...ARE YOU PLANNING TO KEEP THIS UP, ANYWAY?

KLANK

STOP IT, I SAID! DIDN'T YOU HEAR ME?!

OH...
FUMP

THE LAUNDRY ...
FORGET THIS NONSENSE!

NON-SENSE?

NOW I...
...HAVE TO WASH IT AGAIN.

YOU JUST DON'T UNDER-STAND.
A HOUSE-WIFE'S WORK IS NEVER DONE.
THERE'S ALWAYS MORE TO DO.

...
I WORK ALL DAY, THEN I COME HOME TO MORE WORK.
IT'S DEPRESS-ING.
CAN'T YOU SEE?
I'M TIRED.
WELL...
THIS IS THE LIFE YOU CHOSE.
WILL YOU TWO STOP IT?
IT'S DISGRACE-FUL AND I HATE IT!
STOP FIGHT-ING...
...IN FRONT OF YOUR CHILD!
OH DEAR ...
I GUESS ...

...THINGS HAVEN'T BEEN RIGHT...
...FOR A LONG TIME NOW.

IT'S NO FUN AT ALL.
WHY HAVE I BEEN TRYING SO HARD?

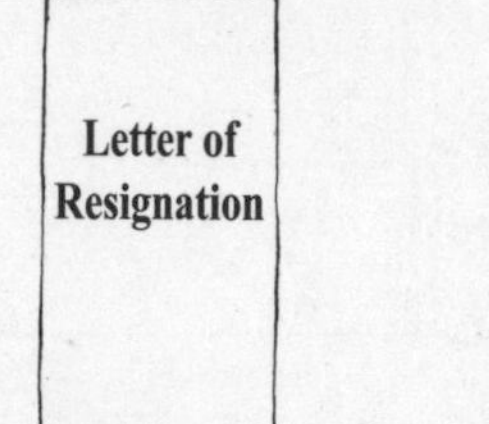
Letter of Resignation

MS. ANZAI, WHAT'S THIS?
I THINK IT'S TIME FOR ME TO QUIT.

I WONDERED WHY YOU ASKED TO SEE ME SO FORMALLY.
BUT I CAN'T ACCEPT THIS UNTIL I'VE CONFERRED WITH THE PRESIDENT.
IT'S NOT A REQUEST.

BLUNTLY

I'LL HAVE MY DESK CLEARED BY TOMOR-ROW.
OH!
WAIT A MINUTE! DON'T BE HASTY!!
I CAN'T WAIT.

BUT YOU CAN'T JUST QUIT. YOU HAVE TO GIVE TWO WEEKS' NOTICE.
LOOK, WHY DON'T YOU TAKE A PAID LEAVE AND THINK IT OVER?

I-I GUESS I COULD DO THAT.

PARDON ME.
KLIK
CONFERENCE ROOM

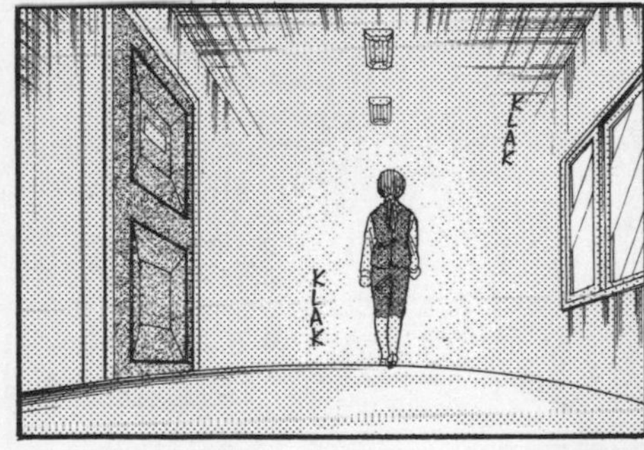
KLAK
KLAK

YACK
LISTEN ...
A GIRL IN ADMINISTRA-TION TOLD ME THE DRAGON LADY TURNED IN HER LETTER OF RESIGNA-TION.
NO WAY!
WORD THAT MS. ANZAI HAD QUIT SOON SPREAD THROUGH THE OFFICE.
EVERYONE KNEW ABOUT IT...

MS. ANZAI...

...EXCEPT ME.

HUH?

GOING HOME ALREADY? IT'S NOT EVEN NOON.

YES.

I WANTED TO ASK YOU FOR SOME REPORT PADS AND PAPER CLIPS, BUT...

...SHALL I ASK ONE OF THE GIRLS?

...

REALLY? THAT'S A SHAME.
IT WON'T BE THE SAME AROUND HERE WITHOUT YOU.
HMPH.
DING
EVERY-ONE'S PROBABLY THRILLED THAT THE OLD HARPY'S LEAVING.
ARE YOU GETTING ON?
NO. I HAVE SOME BUSINESS ON THIS FLOOR.
I SEE.

MS. ANZAI!
WHAT ?!
I WANT YOU TO KNOW...
YOU...
...WERE INDISPENS-ABLE TO THIS COMPANY.
YOU WERE NEEDED.
NEEDED?
WHO ...
... NEEDED ME?

I'VE...
PLIP...
3
4
5
6
TH-THANK YOU...VERY MUCH.
WHO?
...

HE RELEASED ME...
I'VE ALWAYS ...
...WANTED TO HEAR THAT FROM SOMEONE.

I'M...
...ALL RIGHT NOW.
RUSTLE RUSTLE
PHEW ...
KLANK
IT'S BEEN SO LONG SINCE I'VE HAD TIME TO SHOP. I THINK I BOUGHT TOO MUCH.
KLAK
I'M HOME ...
WHAT ?!
TOMP TOMP
MOM?! WHAT ARE YOU DOING HERE?!
WHAT ABOUT WORK?!
OH NO
DO I NEED YOUR PERMISSION?!
WHAT ARE YOU DOING IN THAT APRON ?
HUH ?
SNIFF
SOMETHING'S BURNING.
OH NO!! OKAY, BUT DON'T COME IN HERE!
DON'T !!
Happy Birthday Mom

YOU BURNED IT.
SO? I NEVER CLAIMED TO BE A CHEF.

It didn't rise, either.

TODAY'S MY BIRTHDAY.
I FORGOT ALL ABOUT IT.
I HATE GETTING OLDER, BUT...

THERE WAS NO SCHOOL TODAY. I WAS BORED, SO I DID THE CLEANING AND THE WASH.
I'M BEAT. I'M GONNA TAKE A BATH.

THANK YOU.
SOME-THING JUST CAME OVER ME.
I DON'T KNOW WHY.

STRANGE THINGS SEEM TO HAPPEN IN SERIES.
HERE.

WHAT'S THIS?
IT'S (HIC) SHUSHI ...

HAPPY BIRTHDAY.
WHAT DOES HE TAKE ME FOR?!
HE GETS ME A BOX OF SUSHI HE PICKED UP ON THE WAY HOME FROM THE BAR?
BUT...
ZHUST TELL ME ONE THING...

WHEN ...
...ARE YOU GONNA ASHK ME FOR HELP?
WHAT?

I DON'T GET IT...
WHY WON'T YOU LET ME HELP YOU?

HIC

HIC
I COULD DO THE SHOPPING, OR THE LAUNDRY...
THUD
HIC
DEAR ...
THE TRUTH IS...

...WE WOMEN ARE FOOLS.

TO THINK THAT A LITTLE THING LIKE THIS...
HMPH... HE'S DRUNK! YOU SHOULD JUST SLAP HIM SOBER.
STOP THAT. HE'S TIRED.
TUMP
BUT NOT AS TIRED AS YOU ARE, I BET.
...COULD MAKE ME WEEP WITH HAPPINESS.
SEV-ERAL DAYS LATER
CHIEF !!
I CAN'T TAKE IT!!
WAAAAH
WHY DO I HAVE TO BE THE DRAGON LADY'S REPLACEMENT ?!
SOB
BUT YOU SAID IT WAS EASY.
IT'S NOT EASY, IT'S A NIGHT-MARE!
MS. ANZAI !!
WHAT'S WRONG ?
HUH?

MR. YAMAZAKI, ABOUT THAT LETTER OF RESIGNATION I GAVE YOU...
HUH? YES?
SWUP
RIP
MS. ANZAI?
IF I'M NOT HERE...
...WHO WILL TEACH THESE GIRLS?
YES...
WHO ELSE COULD?
CHIEF OF SOFTWARE PRODUCTION GENERAL AFFAIRS...
...RITSUKO ANZAI, 43 YEARS OLD...
...IS ONCE MORE THE DRAGON LADY.
MS. HIRAMATSU, I CAN'T ALLOW THESE PURCHASES!
How many folders have you bought this month?!
HUH? ARE YOU SERIOUS?

Chapter 50 / The End

Sketches from My Notebooks 4
I did these illustrations in the last year or two. It seems I tend to draw western-looking faces.
H.S. 3.20
H.S. 9.23.

In Loving Memory of Yoshizo

I'm sorry to inform everyone that my rabbit Yoshizo passed away on June 14, 1994. The picture of Yoshizo in volume 8 of *Baby and Me* was from the most recent photograph of her.

I'd stopped drawing Yoshizo. It's been a long time.

At the time, I was in no condition to draw any cartoons. Since then, with the support of those around me, I've been able to overcome my sorrow somewhat.

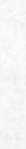

Yoshizo was the one who filled the empty places in my heart when I began my solitary life in Tokyo. She was with me while I worked and suffered in school and as I endured the stresses of life as a cartoonist. Now I must go on living and drawing manga with a hole in my heart. It feels strange. Nothing can replace Yoshizo.

I will end here.

This volume of *Baby and Me* is dedicated to Yoshizo, who watched over me to the end.

October 17, 1994 Marimo

I've ended on a gloomy note.
Sorry. I'm better now.
Really.

BABY & Me

Creator: Marimo Ragawa

SBM Title: *Baby & Me*

Date of Birth: September 21

Blood Type: B

Major Works: *Time Limit*, *Baby & Me*, *N.Y. N.Y.*, and *Shanimuni-Go* (Desperately—Go)

Marimo Ragawa first started submitting manga to a comic magazine when she was 12 years old. She kept up her submissions for four years, but to no avail. She decided to submit her work to the magazine *Hana to Yume*, where she received Top Prize in the Monthly Manga Contest as well as an honorable mention (Kasaku) in the magazine's Big Challenge contest. Her first manga was titled *Time Limit*. *Baby & Me* was honored with a Shogakukan Manga Award in 1995 and was spun off into an anime.

Ragawa's work showcases some very cute and expressive line work along with an incredible ability to depict complex emotions and relationships. Some of her other works include *N.Y. N.Y.* and the tennis manga *Shanimuni-Go*.

Ragawa has two brothers and two sisters.

BABY & ME, Vol. 9
The Shojo Beat Manga Edition

Story & Art by
MARIMO RAGAWA

English Adaptation/Lance Caselman
Translation/JN Productions
Touch-up Art & Lettering/Vanessa Satone
Design/Yuki Ameda
Editor/Shaenon K. Garrity

Editor in Chief, Books/Alvin Lu
Editor in Chief, Magazines/Marc Weidenbaum
VP of Publishing Licensing/Rika Inouye
VP of Sales/Gonzalo Ferreyra
Sr. VP of Marketing/Liza Coppola
Publisher/Hyoe Narita

Printed in Canada.

Published by VIZ Media, LLC
P.O. Box 77010
San Francisco, CA 94107

Shojo Beat Manga Edition
10 9 8 7 6 5 4 3 2 1
First printing, August 2008

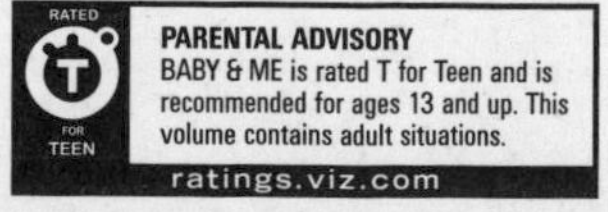
RATED
T
FOR TEEN
PARENTAL ADVISORY
BABY & ME is rated T for Teen and is recommended for ages 13 and up. This volume contains adult situations.
ratings.viz.com

store.viz.com

MeruPuri
Märchen Prince
By Matsuri Hino
Shojo Beat Manga
MeruPuri
Märchen Prince
Story & Art by
Matsuri Hino
All four volumes available now!
Only $8.99
All Airi wants is a cozy home with a loving husband, and school legend has it that the longer one's non-tardy streak is, the better boyfriend one will find. But just when her daily routine is working like clockwork, an occurrence of fairy-tale proportions threatens to disrupt her grand plan...
Buy the complete manga series today!
Shojo Beat
MANGA from the HEART
On sale at:
www.shojobeat.com
Also available at your local bookstore and comic store.
MERUPURI -MÄRCHEN PRINCE- © Matsuri Hino 2002/HAKUSENSHA, Inc.
RATED T FOR TEEN
ratings.viz.com
VIZ media
www.viz.com

Tell us what you think about Shojo Beat Manga!

Our survey is now available online. Go to:

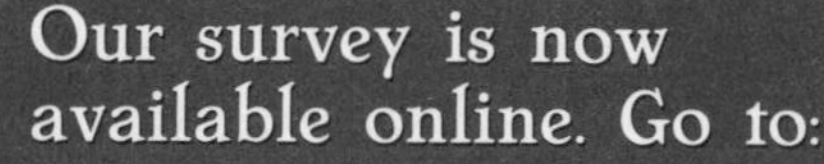

Help us make our product offerings better!